I0753607

BOOK-KEEPING

KEY.

BY IRA MAYHEW, A. M.,

AUTHOR OF "MEANS AND ENDS OF UNIVERSAL EDUCATION."

BOSTON:

CHASE AND NICHOLS,

43 WASHINGTON STREET.

1863.

KEY
TO
MAYHEW'S PRACTICAL BOOK-KEEPING.

In this Key all the "Examples for Practice" occurring in the Book-keeping, and the more difficult problems in "Commercial Calculations," are carefully worked out. By its use Teachers will hence be enabled more readily to detect errors in the work of their classes, than without its aid.

Keys, although generally designed exclusively for *teachers*, are sought, less or more, by *learners* generally. The Author would hence respectfully suggest to those who may use this work, that the thoroughness and ultimate progress of their classes will be *best promoted* when the Key is *least used* by the learner for aid.

After examples have been correctly solved, as an *encouragement* the pupil may with propriety be allowed to compare his work with that in the Key; but rarely (if at all) for the purpose of detecting mistakes. When used as here suggested, classes have not only the satisfaction of solving the examples themselves, and of seeing that their work has been correctly performed, but, while they gain the *discipline* resulting from independent work, they have at the same time the advantage of inspecting the solutions in the Key, which in point of accuracy and neatness they should strive to emulate.

Although prepared with great care, it can hardly be supposed that the Book-keeping and Key are both, or, indeed, either of them, entirely free from mistakes. Should, therefore, persons using them discover material errors in either, they will confer a favor by informing the Author, that the necessary corrections may be made in future editions.

Albion, Mich., 1860. IRA MAYHEW.

Note. **To find the solution of any example in the Book-keeping, look in the Key immediately under the title of the account for the page or pages upon which the example is recorded, which will there be found in the same type with this note.**

KEY.

James Farmer,

In Acct. with Ira Merchant, *Dr.*

		(Page 49.)					
1860							
Jan.	*10*	*To 3½ Yds. Flannel*	*.50*	*1*	*75*		
"	*"*	*" 6 " Calico*	*.15*		*90*		
"	*"*	*" 7¾ " Shirting*	*.16*	*1*	*24*		
May	*4*	*" 1 Hoe, per son John*			*88*		
June	*10*	*" 2 Scythes and Snaths*		*3*	*50*	*8*	*27*
1860		*Cr.*					
Jan.	*10*	*By 9 Bushels Oats*	*.23*	*2*	*07*		
May	*4*	*" 4 Doz. Hens' Eggs*	*.09*		*36*		
June	*10*	*" 8 " do.*	*.08*		*64*		
July	*1*	*" Cash to Balance*		*5*	*20*	*8*	*27*

Isaac Paywell,

In Acct. with Ira Merchant, *Cr.*

1860							
Feb.	*12*	*By 40 Bushels Oats*	*.27*	*10*	*80*		
"	*"*	*" 12 do. Corn*	*.44*	*5*	*28*		
"	*15*	*" 60 do. Wheat*	*.84*	*50*	*40*	*66*	*48*
1860		*Dr.*					
Mar.	*10*	*To 4 Yds. Broadcloth*	*4.50*	*18*	*00*		
"	*"*	*" 16 " Black Silk*	*1.00*	*16*	*00*		
"	*"*	*" Cash to Balance*		*32*	*48*	*66*	*48*

INDEX TO LEDGER B.

(Pages 60 to 71.)

1

Asa P. Leonard Dr.

(Pages 60 to 62.)

1860					
Jan.	4	To 1 Quarter Beef, 150 lbs.	.05	7	50
Feb.	10	" 40 lbs. Pork	.08	3	20
"	15	" 14 Bushels Corn	.45	6	30
May	10	" Plowing Garden		1	75
"	15	" 18 Bushels Potatoes	.35	6	30
June	12	" 250 lbs. Wool	.40	100	00
July	12	" 2 Days' Work with Team	1.75	3	50
Nov.	1	" 14 Weeks' Pasturing Cow	.20	2	80
Dec.	4	" 24 Cords Beech and Maple	1.50	36	00
				167	35

O. D. Knowlton Dr.

1860					
Jan.	4	To 8 Bushels Potatoes	35	2	80
"	"	" 4 do. Corn	.42	1	68
Feb.	10	" 10 do. Potatoes	.35	3	50
"	"	" 12 do. Wheat	.87½	10	50
May	1	" 16 lbs. Butter	.12½	2	00
"	6	" 14 Bushels Corn	.45	6	30
June	10	" 4 do. Potatoes	.35	1	40
July	"	" 10 Tons Hay	4.25	42	50
Sept.	25	" Pasturing 4 Cows 10 Weeks	.20	8	00
"	"	" do. 1 Horse 9 do.	.25	2	25
"	"	" Cash to Balance		2	57
				83	50

Asa P. Leonard Cr.

(Pages 60 to 62.)

1860					
Jan.	4	By 2 lbs. Black Tea	.70	1	40
"	"	" 4 " Coffee	.14		56
"	"	" 25 " Brown Sugar	.10	2	50
"	25	" 3 Gallons Molasses	.44	1	32
Feb.	10	" Cash		40	00
June	12	" 18 Yds. Calico	.15	2	70
"	"	" 3 Papers Pins	.05		15
Dec.	4	" 1 Pr. Kip Brogans		1	25
"	"	" 18 lbs. Rice	.06	1	08
"	"	" 9 " Loaf Sugar	14	1	26
"	"	" 9 Yds. Mer. Sheeting	.09		81
"	29	" Cash to Balance		114	32
				167	35

O. D. Knowlton Cr.

1860				
May	1	By 1 Set Double Harness	30	00
June	10	" 1 Brass-Plated Single Harness	35	00
July	2	" 1 Saddle, Bridle, and Martingale	18	50
			83	50

Isaac Mitchell Dr.

(Pages 62 to 64.)

Date					$	cts
1860						
Jan.	10	To	2½ Doz. Hens' Eggs	.14		35
Feb.	"	"	4 lbs. Butter	.15		60
"	"	"	2 Bushels Wheat	.75	1	50
Mar.	4	"	1 Quarter Beef, 175 lbs.	.05	8	75
May	14	"	18 lbs. Wool	.30	5	40
"	"	"	14 " Butter	.11	1	54
June	10	"	Cash to Balance		8	91
					27	05

Sheep and Wool Account Dr.

Date					$	cts
1859						
June	1	To	Cash for 160 Sheep	1.25	200	00
Dec.	15	"	6½ Mos. Pasturing		31	20
1860						
Mar.	15	"	3 " Foddering		57	60
June	1	"	2½ " Pasturing		12	00
"	"	"	Washing and Shearing per 100,	6.00	9	60
"	"	"	Interest on Cost of 160 Sheep	.07	14	00
"	"	"	Profits on 160 Sheep		153	60
					478	00

Isaac Mitchell Cr.

(Pages 62 to 64.)

1860					
Jan.	1	By 1 Pr. Kip Boots		3	00
"	"	" 1 " Buffalo Overshoes		2	50
Feb.	10	" 1 " India Rubber Overshoes		1	25
"	"	" 1 " Buckskin Mittens			75
Mar.	4	" 1 " Congress Gaiters		3	00
"	"	" 2 " Misses' Gaiters	1.25	2	50
"	"	" 2 " Children's Gloves	.15		30
May	14	" 2 " R. R. Jenny Linds	1.25	2	50
"	"	" 1 " Enamel Gaiters		2	50
"	"	" 6 Linen Hdkfs.	.60	3	60
June	5	" 2 Pr. Boys' Suspenders	.15		30
"	"	" 3 " Mxd. Half Hose	.20		60
"	10	" 1 Leghorn Hat		1	50
"	"	" 2 Pr. Calf Buskins	1.00	2	00
"	"	" 3 " Blk. Cotton Hose	.25		75
				27	05

Sheep and Wool Account Cr.

1860					
June	1	By 600 lbs. Wool	.40	240	00
"	"	" 152 Old Sheep	1.25	190	00
"	"	" 64 Lambs	.75	48	00
				478	00

Henry Webster Dr.

(Pages 64 to 66.)

1860					
Jan.	1	To 15½ lbs. Butter	.14	2	17
"	"	" 25 " Cheese	.08	2	00
"	5	" 40 " Butter	.14	5	60
June	4	" 10 " Linen Rags	.04		40
July	1	" 10 " Butter	.10	1	00
"	"	" 4 Doz. Hens' Eggs	.08		32
"	10	" Cash to Balance			65
				12	14
Sept.	10	To 25 Bushels of Potatoes	.30	7	50
"	"	" 10 lbs. Butter	.12½	1	25
Dec.	12	" 20 Cords Beech and Maple	2.25	45	00
				53	75

Henry Webster Cr.

(Pages 64 to 66.)

1860			$	cts.
Jan.	1	By 1 Family Bible	3	00
"	"	" 1 Webster's Dictionary	3	50
"	"	" 1 Mayhew on Education	1	00
"	10	" 1 Thomson's Higher Arithmetic		75
"	"	" 1 Smith's Arithmetic		50
"	"	" 2 Tower's Intellect. Algebra .37½		75
June	4	" 4 Quires Writing Paper .20		80
"	"	" 2 Tower's Gradual Reader .25		50
"	"	" 2 Spelling Books .10		20
July	1	" 1 Wells' Grammar		38
"	"	" 2 Thomson's Prac. Arith. .38		76
			12	14
Sept.	10	By 2 Quires Writing Paper .25		50
"	"	" 1 Ackerman's Nat. History		50
"	"	" 1 Day-book and 1 Ledger 1.70	3	40
Nov.	1	" 1 Thomson's Higher Arithmetic		75
"	"	" 1 Davies' University do.		75
"	"	" 1 Perkins' Higher do.		75
"	10	" 1 Smith's Astronomy		75
"	"	" 2 Guernsey's History U. S. .62½	1	25
Dec.	15	" 4 Quires Writing Paper .20		80
"	"	" 1 Sons of Temperance Offering	2	25
"	20	" 1 N°. A. Second Class Reader		50
"	"	" 1 Ivory Folder		19
"	"	" 1 Box of Wafers		06
"	"	" Cash to Balance	41	30
			53	75

Pork Account Dr.

(Pages 66 and 67.)

1860					
Sept.	10	To 45 Hogs, weighing 9,856 lbs.	.03	295	68
"	15	" 17 do. do. 4,180 "	.02¾	114	95
"	"	" 900 Bush. Corn	.40	360	00
Oct.	25	" Grinding 280 Bush. Corn	.06	16	80
Dec.	10	" Slaughtering 62 Hogs	.75	46	50
"	12	" Marketing do.	.20	12	40
"	"	" Profit on fattening Pork		123	67
				970	00

Beef Account Dr.

1859					
July	20	To 21 Yoke of Oxen	68.00	1428	00
Aug.	4	" 15 Cows	12.00	180	00
"	10	" 22 do.	12.50	275	00
"	20	" 23 Steers	20.00	460	00
Nov.	1	" 11 Weeks' Pasturing		134	64
"	"	" 100 Loads Pumpkins	.50	50	00
1860					
Feb.	1	" 100 Tons Hay	4.50	450	00
"	"	" 1800 Bushels Corn	.35	630	00
"	"	" Grinding the same	.05	90	00
"	"	" Profit on fattening Beef		164	36
				3862	00

Pork Account Cr. 4

(Pages 66 and 67.)

1860					
Dec.	11	By 750 lbs. Pork for family use	.05	37	50
"	12	" Cash for 18,650 lbs. Pork	.05	932	50
				970	00

Beef Account Cr.

1860					
Feb.	1	By 21 Yoke of Oxen, 980 lbs. each	.05	2058	00
"	"	" 37 Cows 600 " "	.04½	999	00
"	"	" 23 Steers 700 " "	.05	805	00
				3862	00

5 F. M. Granger Dr.

(Pages 68 and 69.)

1860					
Jan.	10	To 10 Cords Wood	2.25	22	50
"	"	" 18 Bushels Potatoes	.30	5	40
"	25	" 20 lbs. Table Butter	.14	2	80
Feb.	10	" 18 Bushels Wheat	1.38	24	84
"	26	" 25 lbs. Table Butter	.15	3	75
Mar.	4	" 2 Tons Hay	4.50	9	00
"	22	" 10 Bushels Potatoes	.35	3	50
June	10	" 10 do. Wheat	1.40	14	00
July	2	" 4 Days' Work with Team	2.00	8	00
"	24	" Pasturing 2 Cows 12 Weeks	.20	4	80
Nov.	25	" 10 Bushels Wheat	1.38	13	80
"	"	" 80 lbs. Butter	.14	11	20
"	"	" 75 " Cheese	.07	5	25
Dec.	1	" 4 Tons Hay	5.00	20	00
"	30	" Cash on Settlement		10	09
"	"	" Note to Balance, at 30 days		50	00
				208	93

F. M. Granger Cr.[5]

(Pages 68 and 69.)

1860					
Jan.	4	By 1 Com. ½ Tug Harness		16	00
"	"	" 3 do. Halters	.75	2	25
"	"	" 2 do. Bridles	.75	1	50
Apr.	10	" 1 do. Saddle		7	00
"	"	" 1 Quilted do.		25	00
"	"	" 1 Pr. Martingales			75
June	6	" 1 Buggy Harness, Blk. Trim.		20	00
"	"	" 1 Com. Single Harness		13	00
"	"	" 2 Bridle Halters	1.20	2	40
July	2	" 1 Plated Buggy Harness		25	00
"	"	" 1 Light Double Harness		30	00
Nov.	15	" Repairing Collars			38
"	"	" 1 Throat-latch			20
"	25	" 1 Hard Leather Trunk		20	00
Dec.	20	" Trimming Buggy		18	00
"	"	" Repairing do. Harness		2	25
"	"	" 1 Long Tug Harness		24	00
"	"	" 1 Bridle Halter		1	20
				208	93

Field of Oats, 5 Acres Dr.

(Pages 69 to 71.)

				$	cts
1860					
Apr.	20	To 5 Days' Plowing	2.00	10	00
"	26	" 18 Bushels Seed	.31	5	58
"	"	" ¾ Day Sowing	1.00		75
"	27	" 2 Days' Harrowing	1.50	3	00
July	20	" 5 do. Harvesting	1.25	6	25
Sept.	22	" Threshing 200 Bushels Oats	.06	12	00
Oct.	26	" Marketing do. do.	.03	6	00
"	"	" Int. on 5 Acres, at $20 per acre	.07	7	00
"	"	" Profit on the Crop		7	42
				58	00

Wheatfield, 60 Acres Dr.

				$	cts
1859					
June	25	To Plowing 60 Acres	1.75	105	00
July	20	" Harrowing do.	.33⅓	20	00
Sept.	10	" Cross Plowing same	1.25	75	00
"	15	" 90 Bush. Seed Wheat	.75	67	50
"	"	" Sowing 60 Acres	.10	6	00
"	"	" Harrowing do.	.75	45	00
1860					
July	10	" Cradling, Binding, and Shocking		60	00
"	14	" Drawing into Barn	.33⅓	20	00
Aug.	1	" Threshing 1500 Bush. Wheat	.10	150	00
"	15	" Marketing 1350 do.	.02	27	00
"	"	" Interest at $20 per Acre	.07	84	00
"	"	" Profit on the Crop		495	50
				1155	00

Field of Oats, 5 Acres Cr.[6]

(Pages 69 to 71.)

1860					
Oct.	26	By 200 Bushels Oats	.25	50	00
"	"	" Straw for Fodder		5	00
"	2	" Cash of Upholsterer for Straw		3	00
				58	00

Wheatfield, 60 Acres Cr.

1860					
Aug.	15	By 100 Bush. Wheat for Seed	.75	75	00
"	"	" 50 " " for family use		37	50
"	"	" Cash for 1350 Bush. Wheat	.75	1012	50
"	"	" Cash of Paper Maker for Straw		20	00
"	"	" Straw for Fodder		10	00
				1155	00

7 **Potatofield, 20 Acres** **Dr.**

(Page 71.)

1860					
May	1	To Plowing 20 Acres	1.50	30	00
"	10	" 225 Bushels Potatoes for Seed	.30	67	50
"	"	" Planting 20 Acres	1.50	30	00
June	25	" Plowing 10 Days	1.25	12	50
"	"	" 30 Days' Work, Hoeing	.75	22	50
Nov.	1	" 70 do. do. Digging	.75	52	50
"	"	" 10 do. do. Marketing	2.00	20	00
"	"	" Int., at $30 per Acre	.07	42	00
"	"	" Profits on the Crop		515	50
				792	50

Potatofield, 20 Acres Cr.[7]

(Page 71.)

1860				
Nov.	1	By 2450 Bushels Potatoes .25	612	50
"	"	" 200 " for Hogs .15	30	00
"	"	" 600 " for home use .25	150	00
			792	50

James Farmer,
In Acct. with Ira Merchant, Dr. Cr.

		(Page 76.)	Dr. $	¢	Cr. $	¢
1860						
Jan.	10	To 3½ Yds. Flannel .50	1	75		
"	"	" 6 " Calico .15		90		
"	"	" 7¾ " Shirting .16	1	24		
"	"	By 9 Bushels Oats .23			2	07
May	4	To 1 Hoe, per son John		88		
"	"	By 4 Doz. Hens' Eggs .09				36
June	10	To 2 Scythes and Snaths	3	50		
"	16	By 8 Doz. Hens' Eggs .08				64
July	1	" Cash to Balance			5	20
			8	27	8	27

Isaac Paywell,
In Acct. with Ira Merchant, Dr. Cr.

			Dr. $	¢	Cr. $	¢
1860						
Feb.	12	By 40 Bushels Oats .27			10	80
"	"	" 12 do. Corn .44			5	28
"	15	" 60 do. Wheat .84			50	40
Mar.	10	To 4 Yds. Broadcloth 4.50	18	00		
"	"	" 16 " Black Silk 1.00	16	00		
"	"	" Cash to Balance	32	48		
			66	48	66	48

INDEX TO LEDGER C.

(Pages 77 to 85.)

A B		N O	
Adams, John	2		
C		**P Q R**	
Cash Account	6		
D E F G		**S**	
Davidson, James	1	*Sheep & Wool Acct.*	11
H		**T**	
Hudson, Otho H.	10	*Tobacco Account 12 Yrs.*	3
		do. do. 23 do.	4
		do. do. 34 do.	5
I		**U V**	
Ingalls, Henry	2		
J K L		**W**	
		Winebibber's Acct. 12 Yrs.	7
		do. do. 23 do.	8
		do. do. 34 do.	9
M		**X Y Z**	
Morgan, O. D.	11		

1 James Davidson Dr. Cr.

(Pages 77 and 78.)

1860				Dr.		Cr.	
Jan.	2	By 18 lbs. Sugar	.08			1	44
"	"	" 15 " Rice	.07			1	05
"	"	" 12 " Loaf Sugar	.14			1	68
Feb.	10	To Cash on Account		4	00		
"	"	By 10 lbs. Codfish	.06				60
"	"	" 2 Galls. Molasses	.44				88
Mar.	4	" 12 lbs. Butter	.15			1	80
"	"	" 10 lbs. Cheese	.08				80
"	24	" 8 " Corn Starch	.11				88
"	"	" 2 " Saleratus	.09				18
"	"	" 4 " Ginger	.10				40
Apr.	12	" 4 Bushels Potatoes	.42			1	68
"	"	" 6 Doz. Eggs	.10				60
"	"	To Cash on Account		4	00		
May	1	By 1 Ham, 18 lbs.	.09			1	62
"	"	" 14 lbs. Corn Meal	.01				14
June	10	" 12 " Rice	.06				72
July	2	" ½ Bush. Potatoes	.50				25
"	"	" 10 lbs. Mackerel	.09				90
Aug.	1	To Cash to Balance		7	62		
				15	62	15	62

Henry Ingalls Dr. Cr. 2

(Pages 78 and 79.)

1860				Dr.		Cr.	
Jan.	4	To 8 Cords Hickory	1.50	12	00		
"	"	By 1 Pr. Kip Boots				4	00
"	"	" 3 " Children's Gaiters				1	80
"	"	" 2 " Boys' Suspenders					28
Apr.	10	" 3 " Children's Gloves					45
"	14	" 4 Linen Hdfs.	.60			2	40
"	"	" 2 Pr. Misses' Gaiters				2	50
May	6	" 1 Leghorn Hat				1	50
"	"	" 2 Palm Leaf Hats	.30				60
"	20	To 80 lbs. Wool	.40	32	00		
"	"	By Cash to Balance				30	47
				44	00	44	00

John Adams Dr. Cr.

1860				Dr.		Cr.	
Jan.	10	By 2 Axes	1.25			2	50
"	"	" 3 Ax Helves	.20				60
Apr.	4	" 3 Shanked Hoes	.65			1	95
"	"	" 1 Welded Eye do.					44
June	10	" 3 Scythes	.88			2	64
"	"	" 2 Scythe Snaths	.75			1	50
"	20	" 20 lbs. Log Chain	.10			2	00
"	"	" 1 Bush Scythe				1	00
July	2	" 1 Grain Cradle				3	00
"	"	" 2 Hay Rakes	.15				30
Sept.	10	To Cash to Balance		15	93		
				15	93	15	93

[3] Tobacco Acct. 12 Yrs. Dr. Cr.

(Pages 79 and 80.)

		Dr.		Cr.	
1841	To Tobacco for one year	37	44		
1842	" Interest on 37.44 one year	2	62		
"	" Tobacco for one year	37	44		
1843	" Interest on 77.50 one year	5	42		
"	" Tobacco for one year	37	44		
1844	" Interest on 120.36 one year	8	43		
"	" Tobacco for one year	37	44		
1845	" Interest on 166.23 one year	11	64		
"	" Tobacco for one year	37	44		
1846	" Interest on 215.31 one year	15	07		
"	" Tobacco for one year	37	44		
1847	" Interest on 267.82 one year	18	75		
"	" Tobacco for one year	37	44		
1848	" Interest on 324.01 one year	22	68		
"	" Tobacco for one year	37	44		
1849	" Interest on 384.13 one year	26	89		
"	" Tobacco for one year	37	44		
1850	" Interest on 448.46 one year	31	39		
"	" Tobacco for one year	37	44		
1851	" Interest on 517.29 one year	36	21		
"	" Tobacco for one year	37	44		
1852	" Interest on 590.94 one year	41	37		
"	" Tobacco for one year	37	44		
"	By Amount to Balance			669	75
		669	75	669	75

Tobacco Acct. 23 Yrs. Dr. Cr.[4]

(Pages 80 and 81.)

Year		Dr. $	¢	Cr. $	¢
1852	To Tobacco for twelve years	669	75		
1853	" Interest on 669.75 one year	46	88		
"	" Tobacco for one year	37	44		
1854	" Interest on 754.07 one year	52	78		
"	" Tobacco for one year	37	44		
1855	" Interest on 844.29 one year	59	10		
"	" Tobacco for one year	37	44		
1856	" Interest on 940.83 one year	65	86		
"	" Tobacco for one year	37	44		
1857	" Interest on 1044.13 one year	73	09		
"	" Tobacco for one year	37	44		
1858	" Interest on 1154.66 one year	80	83		
"	" Tobacco for one year	37	44		
1859	" Interest on 1272.93 one year	89	11		
"	" Tobacco for one year	37	44		
1860	" Interest on 1399.48 one year	97	96		
"	" Tobacco for one year	37	44		
1861	" Interest on 1534.88 one year	107	44		
"	" Tobacco for one year	37	44		
1862	" Interest on 1679.76 one year	117	58		
"	" Tobacco for one year	37	44		
1863	" Interest on 1834.78 one year	128	43		
"	" Tobacco for one year	37	44		
"	By Amount to Balance			2000	65
		2000	65	2000	65

3

5 Tobacco Acct. 34 Yrs. Dr. Cr.

(Page 81.)

Year		Dr.		Cr.	
1863	To Tobacco for twenty-three years	2000	65		
1864	" Interest on 2000.65 one year	140	05		
"	" Tobacco for one year	37	44		
1865	" Interest on 2178.14 one year	152	47		
"	" Tobacco for one year	37	44		
1866	" Interest on 2368.05 one year	165	76		
"	" Tobacco for one year	37	44		
1867	" Interest on 2571.25 one year	179	99		
"	" Tobacco for one year	37	44		
1868	" Interest on 2788.68 one year	195	21		
"	" Tobacco for one year	37	44		
1869	" Interest on 3021.33 one year	211	49		
"	" Tobacco for one year	37	44		
1870	" Interest on 3270.26 one year	228	92		
"	" Tobacco for one year	37	44		
1871	" Interest on 3536.62 one year	247	56		
"	" Tobacco for one year	37	44		
1872	" Interest on 3821.62 one year	267	51		
"	" Tobacco for one year	37	44		
1873	" Interest on 4126.57 one year	288	86		
"	" Tobacco for one year	37	44		
1874	" Interest on 4452.87 one year	311	70		
"	" Tobacco for one year	37	44		
"	By Amount to Balance			4802	01
		4802	01	4802	01

Cash Account Dr. Cr. 6

(Pages 81 and 82.)

1860			Dr.		Cr.	
Jan.	1	To Cash on hand	25	50		
"	29	By 4 Weeks' Board 2.00			8	00
Feb.	27	" 4 " " 2.00			8	00
Mar.	25	" 4 " " 2.00			8	00
Apr.	1	To 1 Quarter's Salary	125	00		
"	10	By 1 Suit of Clothes			30	00
"	24	" 4 Weeks' Board 2.00			8	00
"	"	" 1 Silk Hat			4	00
May	3	" Missionary Subscription			15	00
"	10	" Support of the Ministry			10	00
"	23	" 4 Weeks' Board 2.00			8	00
June	1	" Sundries as per Mem.			4	56
July	4	" Anniversary Expenses			4	57
"	22	" 8 Weeks' Board 2.00			16	00
Aug.	15	To 1½ Quarter's Salary	187	50		
"	25	By 1 Dress and Sundries			12	50
Oct.	1	To ½ Quarter's Salary	62	50		
"	10	By 1 Cow for my Mother			14	00
"	22	" 13 Weeks' Board 2.00			26	00
Nov.	10	" Sundries as per Mem.			7	75
Dec.	31	" 11 Weeks' Board 2.00			22	00
"	"	To 1 Quarter's Salary	125	00		
"	"	By Cash on hand			319	12
			525	50	525	50
1861						
Jan.	1	To Balance	319	12		

7 Wine Account, 12 Ys. Dr. Cr.

(Pages 82 and 83.)

		Dr.		Cr.	
1848	To Wine, Cigars, etc., for one yr.	365	00		
1849	" Interest on 365.00 one year	25	55		
"	" Wine, Cigars, etc., for one yr.	365	00		
1850	" Interest on 755.55 one year	52	89		
"	" Wine, Cigars, etc., for one yr.	365	00		
1851	" Interest on 1173.44 one year	82	14		
"	" Wine, Cigars, etc., for one yr.	365	00		
1852	" Interest on 1620.58 one year	113	44		
"	" Wine, Cigars, etc., for one yr.	365	00		
1853	" Interest on 2099.02 one year	146	93		
"	" Wine, Cigars, etc., for one yr.	365	00		
1854	" Interest on 2610.95 one year	182	77		
"	" Wine, Cigars, etc., for one yr.	365	00		
1855	" Interest on 3158.72 one year	221	11		
"	" Wine, Cigars, etc., for one yr.	365	00		
1856	" Interest on 3744.83 one year	262	14		
"	" Wine, Cigars, etc., for one yr.	365	00		
1857	" Interest on 4371.97 one year	306	04		
"	" Wine, Cigars, etc., for one yr.	365	00		
1858	" Interest on 5043.01 one year	353	01		
"	" Wine, Cigars, etc., for one yr.	365	00		
1859	" Interest on 5761.02 one year	403	27		
"	" Wine, Cigars, etc., for one yr.	365	00		
"	By Amount to Balance			6529	29
		6529	29	6529	29

Wine Account, 23 Ys. Dr. Cr.

(Page 83.)

1859	To Wine, Cigars, etc., for 12 yrs.	6529	29		
1860	" Interest on 6529.29 one year	457	05		
"	" Wine, Cigars, etc., for one yr.	365	00		
1861	" Interest on 7351.34 one year	514	59		
"	" Wine, Cigars, etc., for one yr.	365	00		
1862	" Interest on 8230.93 one year	576	17		
"	" Wine, Cigars, etc., for one yr.	365	00		
1863	" Interest on 9172.10 one year	642	05		
"	" Wine, Cigars, etc., for one yr.	365	00		
1864	" Interest on 10179.15 one yr.	712	54		
"	" Wine, Cigars, etc., for one yr.	365	00		
1865	" Interest on 11256.69 one yr.	787	97		
"	" Wine, Cigars, etc., for one yr.	365	00		
1866	" Interest on 12409.66 one yr.	868	68		
"	" Wine, Cigars, etc., for one yr.	365	00		
1867	" Interest on 13643.34 one yr.	955	03		
"	" Wine, Cigars, etc., for one yr.	365	00		
1868	" Interest on 14963.37 one yr.	1047	44		
"	" Wine, Cigars, etc., for one yr.	365	00		
1869	" Interest on 16375.81 one yr.	1146	31		
"	" Wine, Cigars, etc., for one yr.	365	00		
1870	" Interest on 17887.12 one yr.	1252	10		
"	" Wine, Cigars, etc., for one yr.	365	00		
"	By Amount to Balance			19504	22
		19504	22	19504	22

9 Wine Account, 34 Ys. Dr. Cr.

(Page 83.)

		Dr.		Cr.	
1870	To Wine, Cigars, etc., for 23 yrs.	19504	22		
1871	" Interest on 19504.22 one yr.	1365	30		
"	" Wine, Cigars, etc., for one yr.	365	00		
1872	" Interest on 21234.52 one yr.	1486	42		
"	" Wine, Cigars, etc., for one yr.	365	00		
1873	" Interest on 23085.94 one yr.	1616	02		
"	" Wine, Cigars, etc., for one yr.	365	00		
1874	" Interest on 25066.96 one yr.	1754	69		
"	" Wine, Cigars, etc., for one yr.	365	00		
1875	" Interest on 27186.65 one yr.	1903	07		
"	" Wine, Cigars, etc., for one yr.	365	00		
1876	" Interest on 29454.72 one yr.	2061	83		
"	" Wine, Cigars, etc., for one yr.	365	00		
1877	" Interest on 31881.55 one yr.	2231	71		
"	" Wine, Cigars, etc., for one yr.	365	00		
1878	" Interest on 34478.26 one yr.	2413	48		
"	" Wine, Cigars, etc., for one yr.	365	00		
1879	" Interest on 37256.74 one yr.	2607	97		
"	" Wine, Cigars, etc., for one yr.	365	00		
1880	" Interest on 40229.71 one yr.	2816	08		
"	" Wine, Cigars, etc., for one yr.	365	00		
1881	" Interest on 43410.79 one yr.	3038	76		
"	" Wine, Cigars, etc., for one yr.	365	00		
"	By Amount to Balance			46814	55
		46814	55	46814	55

Otho H. Hudson Dr. Cr. 10

(Page 84.)

1860			Dr.		Cr.	
Jan.	3	By 2 Nail Hammers .50			1	00
"	"	" 1 Cast Steel do.			1	00
"	"	" 2 Hand Saws 2.00			4	00
"	"	" 1 Backed do. Large			2	00
"	"	" 1 do. do. Small			1	25
Feb.	1	" 2 Jack Planes 1.25			2	50
"	"	" 2 Fore Planes 1.25			2	50
"	"	" 2 Long Jointers 1.50			3	00
"	10	" 1 Pr. Match Pl. 1¼ in.			2	00
"	"	" 2 " do. do. 1½ in.			4	50
"	"	" 2 Smoothing do. 1.00			2	00
"	"	To Cash on Account	8	00		
Mar.	20	By one 7 Ft. Cross Cut Saw			4	41
"	"	" do. Mill Saw .94			6	58
"	"	To Cash to Balance	28	74		
			36	74	36	74

Apr.	1	By 2 Bed Cords .25				50
"	"	" 1 Dinner Bell			1	00
"	"	" 1 Clothes Brush				50
"	"	" 1 Nail do.				31
"	"	" 2 Tooth do. .20				40
May	10	" 1 Strainer Milk Pail				60
"	"	" 3 Milk Pans .20				60
"	"	" 1 Wire Sieve				44
"	"	To Cash to Balance	4	35		
			4	35	4	35

11 Sheep and Wool Acct. Dr. Cr.

		(Pages 84 and 85.)	Dr. $	cts.	Cr. $	cts.
1859						
June	5	To 30 Young Sheep 1.25	37	50		
1860						
June	"	" Pasturing and Care 1 yr.	4	80		
"	"	" 30 Bushels of Oats .25	7	50		
"	"	" Washing and Shearing	1	20		
"	"	" Marketing 103 lbs. Wool		50		
"	"	" Int. on 37.50 at 10 per ct.	3	75		
"	"	By 7 lbs. Wool .40			2	80
"	"	" Cash for 103 lbs. .40			41	20
"	"	" 30 Old Sheep 1.50			45	00
"	"	" 27 Lambs 1.25			33	75
		To Profits on 30 Sheep 1 yr.	67	50		
			122	75	122	75

O. D. Morgan Dr. Cr.

			Dr. $	cts.	Cr. $	cts.
1860						
Jan.	25	By 10½ lbs. Sugar .10			1	05
"	"	" 12 " Butter .14			1	68
"	"	" 4 Bushels Potatoes .40			1	60
Feb.	20	" 8 lbs. Rice .06				48
"	"	" 12 " Corn Starch .12½			1	50
May	2	" 8 " Codfish .06				48
"	"	To Cash to Balance	6	79		
			6	79	6	79

ILLUSTRATIVE EXAMPLE.

THIRD FORM OF ACCOUNTS.

(Pages 93 to 102.)

The following are the Transactions upon which the Illustrative Example in the Book-keeping is based. The first of these transactions are given in the Book-keeping as *samples.*

Tuesday, May 1st, 1860.

Transaction 1. I have sold to H. M. Roberts 28 yds. of Sheeting at eight and a half cents a yard, and two pairs of Shoes at one dollar and fifty cents a pair; and I have received from him 22 bushels of Oats at 45 cents a bushel.

Tr. 2. I have received from Isaac Hinman 20 lbs. of Butter at 15 cents a pound, and two Hams, together weighing 44 lbs., at 12½ cents a pound; and I have sold him 3 shanked Hoes at 60 cents each.

Wednesday, May 2d, 1860.

Tr. 3. Have sold to Bronson Fisher 20 Seamless Bags at 22 cents each; one grain Scoop Shovel at one dollar; and 14 lbs. of Rope at 15 cents a pound.

Thursday, May 3d, 1860.

Tr. 4. Have sold to James Ellis one Pocket Compass for 50 cents; 2 pairs of Snuffers at 37½ cents each; and a Pocket Knife worth one dollar.

Tr. 5. N. O. Morehouse has bought of me 2 Brooms at 15 cents each; 7 yards of Gingham at 22 cents a yard; 10¾ yards of Blue Drill at 16 cents a yard; and 2 Scythe Stones at 10 cents a piece.

Friday, May 4th, 1860.

Tr. 6. A. F. Kingsley has bought of me 2 pairs of Spring Dividers at 63 cents a pair; 2 Trunk Locks at 31 cents each; and one Chest Lock worth 44 cents.

(Pages 93 to 102.)

Saturday, May 5th, 1860.

Tr. 7. I have sold to Silas Boomer 2 Dead Locks at $62\frac{1}{2}$ cents each; 2 Cottage Locks at $1.50 each; and 3 Trunk Locks worth 35 cents apiece.

Monday, May 7th, 1860.

Tr. 8. Bronson Fisher has purchased of me 2 Sprinkling Pots at 38 cents each; one Buck Saw worth $1.00; and one Box of 8 x 10 Glass worth $2.25.

Tr. 9. James Sterling has bought of me two Handsaw Files at 10 cents each; one set of Knives and Forks for $1.15; and 12 lbs. of Lead Pipe at 8 cents a pound. I have received of him one quarter of Beef weighing 210 lbs. at 5 cents a pound.

Tuesday, May 8th, 1860.

Tr. 10. I have sold to H. M. Roberts 15 lbs. of Brown Sugar at 10 cents a pound, and $7\frac{3}{4}$ yards of Calico at 16 cents a yard. I have bought of him 14 bushels of Potatoes at 40 cents a bushel.

Thursday, May 10th, 1860.

Tr. 11. I have sold Isaac Hinman 12 yards of Shirting at $12\frac{1}{2}$ c. a yard, and $6\frac{3}{4}$ yds. of Sheeting at 9 c. a yd.

Tr. 12. James Ellis has purchased of me one half-inch Framing Chisel for 50 cents; 2 three-fourth inch Framing Chisels at 75 cents each; and one Cow Bell for 75 cents. He has made some Repairs on my Store, for which he brings in a bill for $4.50, which I place to his credit.

Saturday, May 12th, 1860.

Tr. 13. I have purchased of N. O. Morehouse 6 bushels of Wheat at $1.75 a bushel, and have sold him $10\frac{1}{2}$ lbs. of Cast Steel at 22 cents a pound, and 14 lbs. of German Steel at 15 cents a pound.

(Pages 93 to 102.)

Monday, May 14th, 1860.

Tr. 14. A. F. Kingsley has purchased of me one set of Knives and Forks for $1.25, and one Quart Measure worth 26 cents. I have bought of him 2 cords of Beech Wood at $1.75 per cord.

Tr. 15. Silas Boomer has bought of me 2 Stand Lamps at 37½ cents apiece; 2 Wheel Heads at 25 cents each; and one Pocket Compass for 40 cents.

Thursday, May 17th, 1860.

Tr. 16. James Sterling has bought of me 12 lbs. of Raisins at 12½ cents a pound, and 3½ gallons of Molasses at 56 cents a gallon. I have received of him one quarter of Veal weighing 18 lbs., for which I am to pay him 5 cents a pound.

Saturday, May 19th, 1860.

Tr. 17. H. M. Roberts has purchased of me 2 sets of Coffee Cups at $1.00 a set; one Split Broom worth 25 cents; and 3 common Brooms at 20 cents each.

Monday, May 21st, 1860.

Tr. 18. I have sold Isaac Hinman one set of Knives and Forks for $1.50, and 15 lbs. of Coffee at 18 cents a pound.

Thursday, May 24th, 1860.

Tr. 19. James Ellis has bought of me 2 Pocket Knives for 37½ cents each, and 2 Vest Patterns at $2.25 each, which I have delivered to his son Robert.

Saturday, May 26th, 1860.

Tr. 20. N. O. Morehouse has bought of me one Spice Mill for 75 cents; 2 sets of Knitting Pins at 9 cents a set; and 3 Wheel Heads at 50 cents each. He has brought me 20 lbs. of Butter at 16 cents a pound, and 4 bushels of Wheat at $1.75 a bushel.

(Pages 93 to 102.)

Friday, June 1st, 1860.

Tr. 21. H. M. Roberts has bought of me 14 lbs. of Java Coffee at 20 cents a pound. We have settled, and I have paid him the balance due him in Cash. What was it?

Monday, June 4th, 1860.

Tr. 22. Isaac Hinman has delivered me 75 lbs. of Wool, for which I allow him 42 cents a pound. We settle our account, and I give him my Note for $30.00, payable in thirty days, and the balance due him in Cash. How much Cash do I give him?

Tr. 23. Bronson Fisher has brought me 60 lbs. of Wool, for which I pay him 45 cents a pound. He buys of me 3 Pitchforks at 50 cents each; one Grain Cradle worth $2.25; 4 Hay Rakes at 25 cents each; and I pay him the balance in money. What amount of Cash does he receive on settlement?

Wednesday, June 6th, 1860.

Tr. 24. James Ellis has worked for me two days at $1.50 a day. He has furnished me 200 feet of Pine Boards worth $20.00 per 1000 feet.

Tr. 25. N. O. Morehouse has sent me 40 lbs. of Wool by his hired man, J. Brown. I allow him 40½ cents per pound for his Wool, according to agreement. J. Brown brings an Order from N. O. Morehouse for $6.30, which I pay him in goods. I balance my account with Morehouse, as he requests, and send him the balance in Cash by Brown. What amount of Cash was due him?

Friday, June 8th, 1860.

Tr. 26. I have sold to James Sterling one Umbrella for $1.63, and two Parasols at $1.75 each, which were delivered to his daughter Jane.

(Pages 93 to 102.)

Monday, June 11th, 1860.

Tr. 27. H. Allen brings an Order from A. F. Kingsley requesting me to pay $12.00 in goods to Allen, on Kingsley's account, which I have done.

Tr. 28. Silas Boomer has bought of me two Scythes at $1.13 each; 4 Scythe Stones at 10 cents each; and 2 Snaths at 50 cents each.

Thursday, June 14th, 1860.

Tr. 29. James Sterling has bought of me 24 lbs. of Crushed Sugar at 10 cents a pound, and 2 gallons of Molasses at 56 cents a gallon.

Monday, June 18th, 1860.

Tr. 30. A. F. Kingsley has bought of me 14 lbs. of Java Coffee at 15 cents a pound, and 10 lbs. of Rice at 7 cents a pound. We settle, and he gives me his Note for the balance, my due. What was the sum for which the Note was given?

Wednesday, June 20th, 1860.

Tr. 31. Silas Boomer has bought of me 4 lbs. of Ginger at 15 cents a pound; 6 lbs. of Corn Starch at 12 cents a pound; and 8½ lbs. of Candles at 14 cents a pound. He desires to know how his account stands, and I turn to the Ledger and tell him; but the account is not balanced. Does he owe me or I him? and how much?

Saturday, June 30th, 1860.

Tr. 32. James Ellis calls on me for a settlement, and we examine our accounts, and finding them to agree we balance them and bring down the balance. What is the balance? and in whose favor is it?

Tr. 33. James Sterling also calls upon me for a settlement, and we examine our accounts and balance the books, but without payment. What balance is due? and to whom?

1 # Tuesday, May 1st, 1860.

(Pages 106 and 107.)

	Cash Dr.				
1	To Am't in Safe and Bank			900	00
	—— // ——				
	Bills Receivable, No. 1 Dr.				
2	To James Sill's Note of Jan. 4			225	00
	—— // ——				
	Henry Hart Dr.				
2	To Balance of Old Acct.			75	00
	—— // ——				
	James Farley Dr.				
3	To Balance of Old Acct.			60	00
	—— // ——				
	Isaac Hill Cr.				
3	By Balance of Acct. for Mdse.			260	00
	—— // ——				
	Bills Payable, No. 1 Cr.				
4	By Note to H. Smith for Mdse.			700	00
	—— Wednesday, May 2d. ——				
	Henry Allen Dr.				
	To 80 lbs. Brown Sugar, @ 8½c.	6	80		
4	" 4 bbls. Rock Salt, @ 2.25	9	00		
	" 20 lbs. Java Coffee, @ 20½c.	4	10	19	90
	—— // ——				
	Bills Receivable, No. 2 Dr.				
2	To Mdse. sold Job Otis			75	00
	—— Cr. ——				
2	By Pay't of Sill's Note, No. 1			225	00

Wednesday, May 2d, 1860.

(Pages 106 and 107.)

	Cash — Dr.				
1	To Pay't of Sill's Note, No. 1			225	00
	——— Friday, May 4th. ———				
	O. H. Andrews — Dr.				
	To 3 bbls. Salt, @ 1.25	3	75		
5	" 31½ Yds. Sheeting, @ 8½ c.	2	68	6	43
	——— Cr. ———				
5	By 4 Hams, 70 lbs. @ 14 c.			9	80
	——— " ———				
	A. B. Lincoln — Cr.				
	By 44 Bushels Corn, @ 45 c.	19	80		
6	" 10 do. Wheat, @ 95 c.	9	50	29	30
	——— Dr. ———				
	To 8¾ Yds. Cottonade, @ 24 c.	2	10		
6	" 4 lbs. Black Tea, @ 60 c.	2	40		
	" 4 bbls. Salt, @ 1.25	5	00	9	50
	——— Saturday, May 5th. ———				
	S. O. Jenkins — Dr.				
	To 10 Yds. Calico, @ 11½ c.	1	15		
5	" 12 do. DeLaine, @ 22 c.	2	64		
	" 6 " Franklin Drill, @ 25 c.	1	50	5	29
	——— Cr. ———				
5	By 18 lbs. Butter, @ 20½ c.			3	69
	——— " ———				
	A. C. Morton — Dr.				
6	To 56 lbs. Crushed Sugar, @ 11 c.	6	16		
	" 20½ do. Codfish, @ 6 c.	1	23	7	39

Monday, May 7th, 1860.

	(Pages 107 and 108.)				
	Nathan Powers Dr.				
	To 2 Scythes, @ 1.10	2	20		
7	" 1 Grain Cradle	2	50	4	70
	—— " ——				
	John Ransom Dr.				
	To 2 Pairs of Boots, @ 3.50	7	00		
7	" 8 Milk Pans, @ 40 c.	3	20		
	" 40 Yds. Carpeting, @ 80 c.	32	00	42	20
	—— Tuesday, May 8th. ——				
	John Cooper Dr.				
8	To his Order paid to J. Smith			40	00
	—— " ——				
	Henry Smith Cr.				
8	By Mdse. Invoice No. 1			200	00
	—— " ——				
	Bills Payable, No. 1 Dr.				
4	To Note paid to H. Smith			700	00
	—— " ——				
	Cash Cr.				
1	By Bills Pay. No. 1 taken up			700	00
	—— Thursday, May 10th. ——				
	Isaac Hill Dr.				
3	To Cash on Acct. Mdse.			225	00
	—— " ——				
	Cash Cr.				
1	By Am't paid Isaac Hill	225	00		
	" paid Pedler for Sundries	25	00	250	00

Saturday, May 12th, 1860.

(Pages 108 and 109.)

	Bills Receivable No. 3 Dr.				
2	To Mdse. sold Job Otis S.B. p.4			265	00
	—— // ——				
	Cash Dr.				
1	To Receipts of Drawer . .			25	00
	—— Tuesday, May 15th. ——				
	James Farley Dr.				
3	To 1 De Laine Shawl .	5	00		
	" 30 Yds. Gingham @ 25 c.	7	50	12	50
	Sold to daughter Ellen				
	—— // ——				
	Bills Payable No. 2 Cr.				
4	By Mdse. of H. Smith,				
	Invoice No. 2 . . .			225	00
	—— // ——				
	O. H. Andrews Dr.				
	To one Suit of Clothes . .	34	00		
5	" 1 China Tea Set . .	13	00		
	" 32 Yds. Carpeting @ 80 c.	25	60		
	" 6½ do. Stair Carpet @ 60 c.	3	90	76	50
	—— Friday, May 18th. ——				
	S. O. Jenkins Dr.				
5	To 1 Side Saddle . . .	20	00		
	" 1 Single Harness . .	24	00	44	00
	—— // ——				
	A. B. Lincoln Dr.				
6	To 4 Cast Steel Hoes @ 75 c.	3	00		
	" 2 Grain Cradles @ 2.25	4	50		
	" 4 Hay Rakes @ 15 c.		60	8	10

5 Monday, May 21st, 1860.

	(Page 109.)				
	A. C. Morton Dr.				
6	To 12½ Yds. Gingham @ 30c.	3	75		
	" 3 Pair Cotton Hose @ 28 c.		84		
	" Paid his Order of this date	65	00	69	59
	——— " ———				
	Nathan Powers Dr.				
	To 28 Yds. Sheeting @ 9½ c.	2	66		
7	" 5 " Br. Linen @ 31 c.	1	55		
	" 1¾ Doz. Buttons @ 8 c.		14	4	35
	——— " ———				
	John Ransom Dr.				
	To 7 Yds. Ch. Gingham @ 30 c.	2	10		
7	" 2 Pair Cotton Hose @ 50 c.	1	00		
	" 2 do. ½ Hose @ 31 c.		62	3	72
	Delivered to daughter Mary				
	——— Friday, May 25th. ———				
	Henry Smith Cr.				
8	By Mdse. Invoice No. 3			140	25
	——— Dr. ———				
8	To Cash on Account . .			150	00
	——— " ———				
	Cash Cr.				
1	By Paid H. Smith on Acct.			150	00
	——— " ———				
	John Cooper Dr.				
8	To 30½ Yds. Br. Sheet. @ 10 c.	3	05		
	" 9½ do. Alpaca @ 80 c.	7	60	10	65

Friday, June 1st, 1860.

	(Pages 109 and 110.)				
1	*Cash* Dr.				
	To Rec'd for Goods, S.B. p. 6			275	40
	— // —				
	Bills Receivable No. 4 Dr.				
2	*To Mdse. sold John Wood*				
	S. B. p. 8			350	60
	— // —				
	Henry Hart Dr.				
2	*To 1 Coffee Mill . . .*		88		
	" 1 Pr. Kip Boots . .	4	00		
	" 20 Seamless Bags @ 25 c.	5	00	9	88
	— *Monday, June 4th.* —				
4	*Bills Payable No. 2* Dr.				
	To Pd. Note to H. Smith			225	00
	— // —				
	Cash Cr.				
1	*By my Note, No. 2, taken up*			225	00
	— // —				
	Henry Allen Dr.				
4	*To 4½ Galls. Molasses @ 56 c.*	2	52		
	" 26½ lbs. of Bar Soap @ 8 c.	2	12	4	64
	— *Wednesday, June 6th.* —				
	O. H. Andrews Dr.				
5	*To 3 Yds. Cassimere @ 1.75*	5	25		
	" 8 " R. Sheeting @ 37½ c.	3	00	8	25
	— // —				
	Henry Smith Cr.				
8	*By Bill Mdse. Invoice No. 4*			280	00

Saturday, June 9th, 1860.

	(Page 110.)				
	Bills Receivable No. 4 Cr.				
2	By Pay't of John Wood's Note			350	60
	—— " ——				
	Cash Dr.				
1	To Pay't of John Wood's				
	Note No. 4			350	60
	—— " ——				
	James Farley Dr.				
	To 44½ lbs. Sugar @ 10 c.	4	45		
3	" 3 lbs. Saleratus @ 8 c.		24		
	" 27 Yds. Cotton Cloth @ 9 c.	2	43	7	12
	—— Tuesday, June 12th. ——				
	Isaac Hill Cr.				
3	By Bill Mdse. Invoice No. 5			275	66
	—— " ——				
2	Bills Receivable No. 3 Cr.				
	By Pay't of Job Otis's Note			265	00
	—— " ——				
	Cash Dr.				
1	To P't of J. Otis's Note No. 3			265	00
	—— Thursday, June 14th. ——				
	Henry Allen Dr.				
4	To 8 lbs. Raisins @ 18¾ c.	1	50		
	" 41½ Yds. Sheeting @ 10 c.	4	15	5	65
	—— " ——				
	S. O. Jenkins Dr.				
5	To 8 lbs. of Java Coffee @ 18¾ c.	1	50		
	" 25 lbs. Coffee Sugar @ 10 c.	2	50	4	00

Saturday, June 16th, 1860. 8

(Pages 110 and 111.)

1	Cash Dr.				
	To Receipts of Drawer .			24	50
	——— // ———				
	Henry Hart Dr.				
2	To 1 Bbl. Flour . . .	6	50		
	" 40 lbs. Sugar @ 9½ c. .	3	80	10	30
	——— // ———				
	Bills Payable No. 3 Cr.				
4	By Bill Mdse. Invoice No. 6			360	00
	——— Monday, June 18th. ———				
	Cash Dr.				
1	To Mdse. sold as per S. B. p. 10			235	50
	——— // ———				
	Bills Receivable No. 5 Dr.				
2	To Mdse. sold John Wood				
	S. B. p. 12			269	50
	——— // ———				
3	Isaac Hill Dr.				
	To my Note to Bal. Acct.			310	66
	——— // ———				
4	Bills Payable No. 4 Cr.				
	By my Note to I. Hill .			310	66
	——— Friday, June 22d. ———				
6	A. B. Lincoln Dr.				
	To 2 Bbls. Coarse Salt @ 2.30			4	60
	——— // ———				
6	A. C. Morton Dr.				
	To his Order Paid to F. Sill			25	00

9 Monday, June 25th, 1860.

(Pages 111 and 112.)

2	Bills Receivable No. 2 Cr.				
	By Pay't of Job Otis's Note			75	00
	——— " ———				
1	Cash Dr.				
	To Pay't of Job Otis's Note				
	No. 2			75	00
	—— Wednesday, June 27th. ——				
6	A. C. Morton Dr.				
	To 6¾ Yds. Sheeting @ 9 c.		61		
	" 2¾ " Cassimere @ 2.00	5	50	6	11
	——— " ———				
7	Nathan Powers Dr.				
	To 3½ Yds. Blk. Cambric @ 12 c.		42		
	" 2 Linen Hdkfs. @ 35 c.		70		
	" 12 lbs. Java Coffee @ 17 c.	2	04	3	16
	—— Friday, June 29th. ——				
8	John Cooper Dr.				
	To 8 lbs. Brown Sugar @ 10 c.		80		
	" 12 " Candles @ 14½ c.	1	74	2	54
	——— " ———				
7	John Ransom Dr.				
	To 3 Pr. Cotton Hose @ 50 c.	1	50		
	" 2 " Kid Buskins @ 1.50	3	00		
	" 1⅔ Doz. Buttons @ 6 c.		10	4	60
	——— " ———				
2	Henry Hart Cr.				
	By 4 Doz. Hens' Eggs @ 16 c.		64		
	" 8 Hams, 160 lbs. @ 12 c.	19	20	19	84

PROOF OF POSTINGS AND BALANCES.

(Pages 105 to 112.)

Day Book Drs. and Crs. June 30th, 1860.

Dr. Sums.			Cr. Sums.		
Dr. Sum on Page 1	1354	90	Cr. Sum on Page 1	1185	00
" " 2	253	61	" " 2	42	79
" " 3	1011	90	" " 3	1150	00
" " 4	431	10	" " 4	225	00
" " 5	238	31	" " 5	290	25
" " 6	873	77	" " 6	505	00
" " 7	632	37	" " 7	981	26
" " 8	880	06	" " 8	670	66
" " 9	91	41	" " 9	94	84
			Balance . .	712	63
	5767	43		5767	43

Dr. *Ledger Balances, June 30th*, 1860. *Cr.*

Dr.			Cr.		
Cash, p. 1	1051	00	Bills Payable, p. 4	670	66
Bills Receivable, 2	269	50	A. B. Lincoln, p. 6	7	10
Henry Hart, p. 2	75	34	Henry Smith, p. 8	470	25
James Farley, p. 3	79	62	Balance . .	712	63
Henry Allen, p. 4	30	19			
O. H. Andrews, 5	81	38			
S. O. Jenkins, p. 5	49	60			
A. C. Morton, p. 6	108	09			
Nathan Powers, 7	12	21			
John Ransom, p. 7	50	52			
John Cooper, p. 8	53	19			
	1860	64		1860	64

Monday, July 2d, 1860.

Fol.	Particulars	$	c.	$	c.
	(Pages 113 and 114.)				
	Isaac Hill Cr.				
3	By Cash to buy Wool . .			1200	00
	———— // ————				
	Cash Dr.				
1	To Isaac Hill on Wool Acct.			1200	00
	———— // ————				
	Bills Receivable No. 5 Cr.				
2	By Pay't John Wood's Note			269	50
	———— // ————				
	Cash Dr.				
1	To Pay't of John Wood's Note				
	No. 5			269	50
	—— Tuesday, July 3d. ——				
	James Farley Dr.				
3	To 2 Straw Hats @ 37½ c.		75		
	" 4 lbs. Corn Starch @ 12 c.		48	1	23
	———— Cr. ————				
3	By 190 lbs. Wool @ 40 c.			76	00
	—— Thursday, July 5th. ——				
	Henry Allen Dr.				
4	To 1 Grain Cradle . . .	2	50		
	" 2 Scythes @ 88 c. . .	1	76	4	26
	———— Cr. ————				
4	By 165 lbs. Wool @ 40 c.			66	00
	———— // ————				
	Nathan Powers Dr.				
7	To 4 lbs. Wool Twine @ 16 c.		64		
	" 18 " Brown Sugar @ 9 c.	1	62	2	26

Friday, July 6th, 1860.

(Pages 114 and 115.)

Folio	Particulars	$	c.	$	c.
	John Ransom Dr.				
7	To 4 lbs. Wool Twine @ 16 c.		64		
	" 2 Pr. Sheep Shears @ 1.25	2	50	3	14
	——Cr.——				
7	By 24 lbs. Butter @ 14 c.			3	36
	—— Monday, July 9th. ——				
	Nathan Powers Cr.				
7	By 245 lbs. Wool @ 42 c. .			102	90
	——Dr.——				
	To 2 Cedar Pails @ 75 c. .	1	50		
7	" 10½ lbs. Sugar @ 10 c. .	1	05		
	" 1 Doz. Blue Plates .	1	00	3	55
	—— Thursday, July 12th. ——				
	Cash Cr.				
1	By 540 lbs. Wool of White @ 43 c.	232	20		
	" 600 " do. " Brown @ 43 c.	258	00	490	20
	—— " ——				
	Isaac Hill Cr.				
3	By Cash to buy Wool . .			1800	00
	—— " ——				
	Cash Dr.				
1	To Isaac Hill on Wool Acct.			1800	00
	—— " ——				
	A. B. Lincoln Cr.				
6	By 250 lbs. Wool @ 44 c. .	110	00		
	" 18 " Butter @ 14 c. .	2	52		
	" 4 Doz. Hens' Eggs @ 15 c.		60	113	12

12 Saturday, July 14th, 1860.

L.F.	Particulars	$	¢	$	¢
	(Page 115.)				
8	John Cooper Cr.				
	By 425 lbs. Wool @ 45 c. .			191	25
	——— // ———				
5	O. H. Andrews Cr.				
	By 980 lbs. Wool @ 45 c. .			441	00
	——— Dr. ———				
	To 1 Remnant of Edging .		25		
5	" $9\frac{5}{16}$ lbs. Codfish @ 7 c. .		65		
	" 32 Yds. Calico @ 15 c. .	4	80	5	70
	——— Monday, July 16th. ———				
8	Henry Smith Cr.				
	By Bill Mdse. Invoice No. 7			475	00
	——— // ———				
6	A. C. Morton Cr.				
	By 440 lbs. Wool @ 42 c. .			184	80
	——— Dr. ———				
	To 14 lbs. Java Coffee @ 15 c.	2	10		
6	" 25 lbs. Brown Sugar @ 9 c.	2	25		
	" Cash to Balance Acct.	72	36	76	71
	——— // ———				
1	Cash Cr.				
	By Bal. A. C. Morton's Acct.			72	36
	——— // ———				
3	James Farley Cr.				
	By 460 lbs. Wool @ 45 c. .			207	00
	——— Dr. ———				
3	To my Note, No. 5, to Bal. Acct.			202	15

(Pages 115 and 116.)

4	Bills Payable — Cr.				
	By Note to J. Farley to Bal. Acct.			202	15
	—— Wednesday, July 18th. ——				
4	Bills Payable No. 4 — Dr.				
	To Note Paid to J. Hill.			310	66
	—— // ——				
1	Cash — Cr.				
	By my Note, No. 4, taken up			310	66
	—— Friday, July 20th. ——				
4	Bills Payable No. 3 — Dr.				
	To Note Paid to S. Brown			360	00
	—— // ——				
1	Cash — Cr.				
	By my Note, No. 3, taken up			360	00
	—— // ——				
2	Henry Hart — Cr.				
	By 196 lbs. Wool @ 40 c. .			78	40
	—— Dr. ——				
2	To 19⅛ lbs. Coffee @ 16 c. .			3	06
	—— Saturday, July 21st. ——				
5	S. O. Jenkins — Cr.				
	By 450 lbs. Wool @ 42 c. .			189	00
	—— // ——				
	Cash — Cr.				
1	By 680 lbs. Wool @ 40 c. .	272	00		
	" 951 " do. @ 40 c. .	380	40		
	" 720 " do. @ 40½ c. .	291	60	944	00

Monday, July 23d, 1860.

(Pages 116 and 117.)

	Isaac Hill Dr.				
3	To 7281 lbs. Wool, cost .	3080	55		
	" my Commission @ 1 c. .	72	81	3153	36
	—— Tuesday, July 24th. ——				
	Henry Allen Dr.				
	To 10 Gals. Molasses @ 44 c.	4	40		
4	" 45 lbs. Brown Sugar @ 10 c.	4	50		
	" Cash to Balance Acct. .	22	65	31	55
	—— " ——				
	Cash Cr.				
1	By Pd. H. Allen to Bal. Acct.			22	65
	—— Wednesday, July 25th. ——				
5	O. H. Andrews Dr.				
	To Cash to Bal. Acct. .			353	92
	—— " ——				
	Cash Cr.				
1	By Paid O. H. Andrews to Balance Acct. . . .			353	92
	—— Thursday, July 26th. ——				
3	Isaac Hill Cr.				
	By Cash to Bal. Wool Acct.			153	36
	—— " ——				
	Cash Dr.				
1	To Balance of Wool Acct.			153	36
	—— Friday, July 27th. ——				
	S. O. Jenkins Dr.				
5	To 1 Grain Scoop Shovel.	1	25		
	" 3 Gals. Lamp Oil @ 1.75	5	25	6	50

	(Page 117.)		
2	Bills Receivable No. 6 Dr. To Bill Mdse. to James Sill S. B. p. 18		254 60
	—— // ——		
8	John Cooper Dr. To Cash to Balance Acct. .		138 06
	—— // ——		
1	Cash Cr. By Pd. J. Cooper to Bal. Acct.		138 06
	—— Monday, July 30th. ——		
8	Henry Smith Dr. To his Order to Jenkins .		200 00
	—— // ——		
5	S. O. Jenkins Cr. By Henry Smith's Order .		200 00

PROOF OF POSTINGS AND BALANCES.

(Pages 113 to 118.)

Day Book Drs. and Crs., July 31st, 1860.

Dr. Sums.			Cr. Sums.		
Balance June 30th	$712	63	Cr. Sum on P. 10	$1611	50
Dr. Sum on P. 10	1477	25	" " 11	2509	58
" " 11	1806	69	" " 12	1571	41
" " 12	284	56	" " 13	2084	21
" " 13	673	72	" " 14	529	93
" " 14	3698	69	" " 15	338	06
" " 15	592	66	Balance . .	601	51
	9246	20		9246	20

Dr. *Ledger Balances, July 31st, 1860.* *Cr.*

Dr.			Cr.		
Cash, p. 1	1782	01	Bills Payable, p. 4	202	15
Bills Receivable, 2	254	60	S. O. Jenkins, p. 5	332	90
John Ransom, p. 7	50	30	A. B. Lincoln, p. 6	120	22
			Nathan Powers, 7	84	88
			Henry Smith, p. 8	745	25
			Balance . .	601	51
	2086	91		2086	91

INDEX TO LEDGER E.

(Pages 106 to 121.)

1 **Dr.** **Cash** **Cr.**

(Pages 106 to 121.)

1860.						1860.					
May	1	To D.	1	900	00	May	8	By D.	3	700	00
"	2	"	2	225	00	"	10	"	3	250	00
"	12	"	4	25	00	"	25	"	5	150	00
June	1	"	6	275	40	June	4	"	6	225	00
"	9	"	7	350	60	"	30	Balance		1051	00
"	12	"	7	265	00						
"	16	"	8	24	50						
"	18	"	8	235	50						
"	25	"	9	75	00						
				2376	00					2376	00

Dr. **Cash** **Cr.**

1860.						1860.					
July	2	Bal.		1051	00	July	12	By D.	11	490	20
"	2	To D.	10	1200	00	"	16	"	12	72	36
"	2	"	10	269	50	"	18	"	13	310	66
"	12	"	11	1800	00	"	20	"	13	360	00
"	26		14	153	36	"	21	"	13	944	00
						"	24	"	14	22	65
						"	25	"	14	353	92
						"	28	"	15	138	06
						"	31	Balance		1782	01
				4473	86					4473	86
Aug.	1	Bal.		1782	01						

Dr. Bills Receivable Cr. 2

(Pages 106 to 121.)

				$	cts.					$	cts.
1860.						1860.					
May	1	No. 1	1	225	00	May	2	No. 1	1	225	00
"	2	" 2	1	75	00	June	9	" 4	7	350	60
"	12	" 3	4	265	00	"	12	" 3	7	265	00
June	1	" 4	6	350	60	"	25	" 2	9	75	00
"	18	" 5	8	269	50	"	30	Balance		269	50
				1185	10					1185	10
July	2	Bal.		269	50	July	2	No. 5	10	269	50
"	28	No. 6	15	254	60	"	31	Balance		254	60
				524	10					524	10
Aug.	1	Bal.		254	60						

Dr. Henry Hart Cr.

				$	cts.					$	cts.
1860.						1860.					
May	1	Bal.	1	75	00	June	29	By D.	9	19	84
June	1	To D.	6	9	88	"	30	Balance		75	34
"	16	"	8	10	30						
				95	18					95	18
July	2	Bal.		75	34	July	20	By D.	13	78	40
"	20	To D.	13	3	06						
				78	40					78	40

3 Dr. **James Farley** Cr.

(Pages 106 to 121.)

1860.				$	¢	1860.				$	¢
May	1	Bal.	1	60	00	June	30	Balance		79	62
"	15	To D.	4	12	50						
June	9	"	7	7	12						
				79	62					79	62
July	2	Bal.		79	62	July	3	By D.	10	76	00
"	3	To D.	10	1	23	"	16	"	12	207	00
"	16	"	12	202	15						
				283	00					283	00

Dr. **Isaac Hill** Cr.

1860.				$	¢	1860.				$	¢
May	10	To D.	3	225	00	May	1	Bal.	1	260	00
June	18	"	8	310	66	June	12	By D.	7	275	66
				535	66					535	66
July	23	To D.	14	3153	36	July	2	By D.	10	1200	00
						"	12	"	11	1800	00
						"	26	"	14	153	36
				3153	36					3153	36

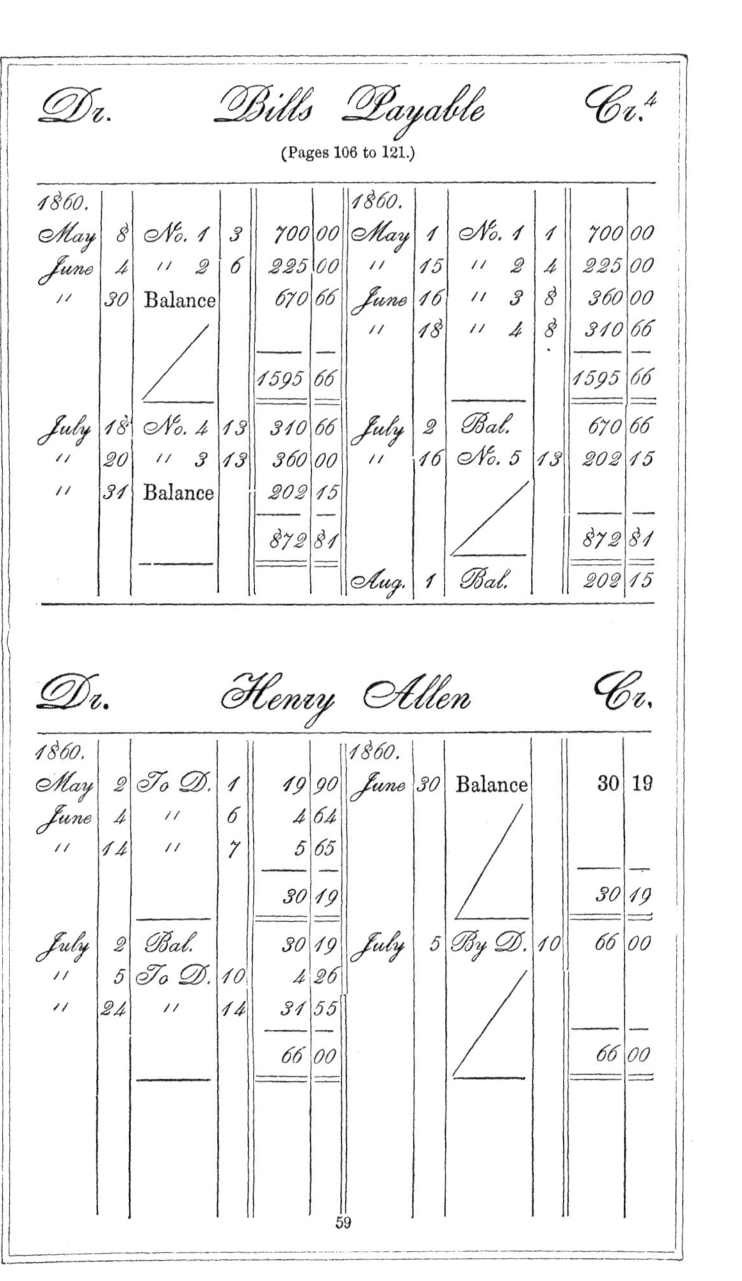

Dr. Bills Payable Cr. 4

(Pages 106 to 121.)

1860.						1860.					
May	8	No. 1	3	700	00	May	1	No. 1	1	700	00
June	4	" 2	6	225	00	"	15	" 2	4	225	00
"	30	Balance		670	66	June	16	" 3	8	360	00
						"	18	" 4	8	310	66
				1595	66					1595	66
July	18	No. 4	13	310	66	July	2	Bal.		670	66
"	20	" 3	13	360	00	"	16	No. 5	13	202	15
"	31	Balance		202	15						
				872	81					872	81
						Aug.	1	Bal.		202	15

Dr. Henry Allen Cr.

1860.						1860.					
May	2	To D.	1	19	90	June	30	Balance		30	19
June	4	"	6	4	64						
"	14	"	7	5	65						
				30	19					30	19
July	2	Bal.		30	19	July	5	By D.	10	66	00
"	5	To D.	10	4	26						
"	24	"	14	31	55						
				66	00					66	00

5 Dr. O. H. Andrews Cr.

(Pages 106 to 121.)

1860.						1860.					
May	4	To D.	2	6	43	May	4	By D.	2	9	80
"	15	"	4	76	50	June	30	Balance		81	38
June	6	"	6	8	25						
				91	18					91	18
July	2	Bal.		81	38	July	14	By D.	12	441	00
"	14	To D.	12	5	70						
"	25	"	14	353	92						
				441	00					441	00

Dr. S. O. Jenkins Cr.

1860.						1860.					
May	5	To D.	2	5	29	May	5	By D.	2	3	69
"	18	"	4	44	00	June	30	Balance		49	60
June	14	"	7	4	00						
				53	29					53	29
July	2	Bal.		49	60	July	21	By D.	13	189	00
"	27	To D.	14	6	50	"	30	"	15	200	00
"	31	Balance		332	90						
				389	00					389	00
						Aug.	1	Bal.		332	90

Dr. A. B. Lincoln Cr. 6

(Pages 106 to 121.)

1860.						1860.					
May	4	To D.	2	9	50	May	4	By D.	2	29	30
"	18	"	4	8	10						
June	22	"	8	4	60						
"	30	Balance		7	10						
				29	30					29	30
July	31	Balance		120	22	July	2	Bal.		7	10
						"	12	By D.	11	113	12
				120	22					120	22
						Aug.	1	Bal.		120	22

Dr. A. C. Morton Cr.

1860.						1860.					
May	5	To D.	2	7	39	June	30	Balance		108	09
"	21	"	5	69	59						
June	22	"	8	25	00						
"	27	"	9	6	11						
				108	09					108	09
July	2	Bal.		108	09	July	16	By D.	12	184	80
"	16	To D.	12	76	71						
				184	80					184	80

7 Dr. **Nathan Powers** Cr.

(Pages 106 to 121.)

1860.				$	¢	1860.				$	¢
May	7	To D.	3	4	70	June	30	Balance		12	21
"	21	"	5	4	35						
June	27	"	9	3	16						
				12	21					12	21
July	2	Bal.		12	21	July	9	By D.	11	102	90
"	5	To D.	10	2	26						
"	9	"	11	3	55						
"	31	Balance		84	88						
				102	90					102	90
						Aug.	1	Bal.		84	88

Dr. **John Ransom** Cr.

1860.				$	¢	1860.				$	¢
May	7	To D.	3	42	20	June	30	Balance		50	52
"	21	"	5	3	72						
June	29	"	9	4	60						
				50	52					50	52
July	2	Bal.		50	52	July	6	By D.	11	3	36
"	6	To D.	11	3	14	"	31	Balance		50	30
				53	66					53	66
Aug.	1	Bal.		50	30						

Dr. John Cooper Cr.

(Pages 106 to 121.)

1860.				$	¢	1860.				$	¢
May	8	To D.	3	40	00	June	30	Balance		53	19
"	25	"	5	10	65						
June	29	"	9	2	54						
				53	19					53	19
July	2	Bal.		53	19	July	14	By D.	12	191	25
"	28	To D.	15	138	06						
				191	25					191	25

Dr. Henry Smith Cr.

1860.				$	¢	1860.				$	¢
May	25	To D.	5	150	00	May	8	By D.	3	200	00
June	30	Balance		470	25	"	25	"	5	140	25
						June	6	"	6	280	00
				620	25					620	25
July	30	To D.	15	200	00	July	2	Bal.		470	25
"	31	Balance		745	25	"	16	By D.	12	475	00
				945	25					945	25
						Aug.	1	Bal.		745	25

COMPUTATION OF TIME.

EXAMPLE IV.

(Page 135.)

Years.		Mos.		Days.	
1857	"	8	"	8	Date of 1st Payment.
1857	"	2	"	8	Date of the Note.
0	"	6	"	0	Time to the 1st Payment.
1858	"	5	"	18	Date of 2d Payment.
1857	"	8	"	8	Date of 1st Payment.
0	"	9	"	10	Time from 1st to 2d Payment.
1859	"	2	"	24	Date of 3d Payment.
1858	"	5	"	18	Date of 2d Payment.
0	"	9	"	6	Time from 2d to 3d Payment.
1860	"	1	"	9	Date of taking up Note.
1859	"	2	"	24	Date of 3d Payment.
0	"	10	"	15	Time from 3d Payment.

Operation.

Principal, ...		$1285.00
Interest to 1st payment, Sept. 8th, (6 mos.,) . .		44.975
Amount due on note Sept. 8th, ...		$1329.975
Deduct payment, (which is *more* than interest,)		85.50
Balance after 1st payment. *New Principal,* .		$1244.475
Interest on *New Prin.* to 2d payment, June 18th, (9 mos. and 10 days,)	$67.755	
Payment is *less* than interest due, . .	30.25	
Interest *unpaid* June 18th, 1858, . . .	$37.505	
Interest on *Last Prin.* from June 18th to March 24th, 1859, 9 mos. 6 days,	66.786	104.291
Amount due March 24th, 1859, ...		$1348.766
Deduct payment, (now *more* than interest,) . .		250.00
Balance after 3d payment. *New Principal,* .		$1098.766
Interest on last *Prin.* to Feb. 9th, (10 mos. 15 ds.,)		67.299
Amount due on taking up note Feb. 9th, 1860,		$1166.065

EXAMPLE V.

(Page 138.)

Face of Note, dated July 2d, ...	$800.00
Interest on same 2 mos. till Sept. 2d, when it is due and may be paid, which Bank allows,	8.00
Amount due on Note Sept. 2d, ...	$808.00
Discounted Aug. 2d. The Bank charges interest 1 mo. 3 ds., (grace being allowed,) amounting to,	4.444
Net proceeds of Note, August 2d, ...	$803.556

EXAMPLE VI.

Interest of $1 for 30 days $= \frac{7}{12} = \frac{70}{120}$ of 1 c.
Int. for 3 *days' grace* $= \frac{1}{10}$ of $\frac{7}{12} = \frac{7}{120}$ of 1 c. } $= \frac{77}{120}$ of 1 c.

$1, or 100 c. $- \frac{77}{120} = 99\frac{43}{120}$ c. = Present worth of $1. Hence, (Art. 186 of Book-keeping,)

$1000.00 $\div 99\frac{43}{120} =$ $1006.458+ = Face of Note required.

EXAMPLE VII.

Amount of debt, ...	$1500.00
Cash to apply on same, ...	900.00
Present value of the required Note, ...	$600.00

Interest of $1 for 9 mos. @ 8 % = 6 cents.

Present worth of $1 due 9 mos. hence = 100 c. — 6 c. = 94 c.

And $600.00 ÷ .94 = $638.299 nearly. *Ans.*

EXAMPLE VIII.

Interest of $1 for 4 months @ 6 % = 2 cents =	.02
Int. for 3 *days' grace* $= \frac{1}{10}$ of $\frac{1}{4}$ of 2 c. $= \frac{2}{40} = \frac{1}{20}$ c. =	.0005
Interest 4 months and 3 days @ 6 % =	.0205

Now $1.00 — $.0205 = $.9795, and

$4268.00 ÷ .9795 = $4357.325. *Ans.*

EXAMPLE VI.

(Page 140.)

Proceeds of Draft on St. Louis for $1260 @ *discount* of $2\frac{1}{4}$ % = $1231.65.

Premium on Boston Draft at $\frac{3}{4}$ of 1 % = $9.24 nearly.

$1231.65 — $9.24 = $1222.41. Am't of Draft on Boston.

EXAMPLE V.

(Pages 145 and 146.)

This example may be solved in several ways.

1st. In the solution here given we compute the time for the Dr. side of the account from the *date of the first bill,* to the time when each of the several bills *becomes due;* and then make the calculation. (Art. 194 of Book-keeping.)

Date.	Amount.		Time.		Product.
Jan. 16.	560	×	120 d.	=	67200
Feb. 1.	380	×	135	=	51300
Feb. 16.	340	×	150	=	51000
April 21.	400	×	185	=	74000
	1680				243000

Now 243000 ÷ 1680 = 145 days, (nearly,) or 4 months 25 days, which added to Jan. 16th, makes *June 11th,* as the time when the several bills *average due.* (Art. 178.)

We in like manner compute the time for the Cr. side of the account from the *date of the first payment,* to the time when *each payment was made.*

Date.	Amount.		Time.		Product.
March 25.	$450	×	00 d.	=	00
May 20.	430	×	55	=	23650
	880				23650

Now 23650 ÷ 880 = 27 days, (nearly,) which, added to March 25th, makes April 22d, as the *average time* for the payment of the $880.00.

(Pages 145 and 146 continued.)

We next subtract April 22d from June 11th, which gives 1mo. 19d., or 49 days. Now, $880 \times 49 = 43120$; and $43120 \div 800 = 54$ days, (nearly,) or 1mo. 24d. (Art. 196, Ex. 3.) Now 1mo. 24d. added to June 11th, gives August 5th, as the time when the *balance* of the account ($800) should be paid. My *gain* from the use of $880 the 49 days *before* it was due, will just equal my *loss* of the use of $800 (the *balance*) for 54 days *after* it is due.

2d. We might have made the same computation by *interest*, which some prefer. In this case, instead of obtaining the *products*, as above, by multiplying the several amounts into the time they had to run, we should compute the *interest* on the several sums for the same time, and then ascertain how long it would take the sum total, or the required *balance*, as the case may be, *to earn the same interest*, which would give the same result as that obtained by the method we have adopted.

EXAMPLE IN PARTNERSHIP.

(Page 147.)

A has in trade:					B has in trade:				
Amount.		Time.		Product.	Amount.		Time.		Product.
5000	×	4	=	20000	8000	×	6	=	48000
7000	×	20	=	140000	5000	×	18	=	90000
Sum of A's products,				160000	Sum of B's products,				138000

Now 160000 = sum of A's products of amount into time,
And 138000 = sum of B's products of amount into time,
And 298000 = sum total of products of amount into time.

$$298000 : \begin{cases} 160000 \\ 138000 \end{cases} : : 298 : \begin{cases} 1600 = \text{A's share of gain.} \\ 1380 = \text{B's share of gain.} \end{cases}$$

Journal B.—Double Entry.

(Pages 198 and 199.)

	Wednesday, February 1st, 1860.				
	Sundries Dr.				
1	*Merchandise*	1471	00		
2	*Cash*	7812	00		
3	*S. C. Wood & Co.* . . .	2650	00		
4	*James Armitage*	2060	00		
3	**1** *To Stock*			13993	00
	——— // ———				
3	*Stock* Dr.	1115	00		
5	*To Clark & Smith* .			500	00
6	**2** // *Hill & Wright* .			615	00
	——— *Feb. 2d.* ———				
3	*S. C. Wood & Co.* Dr.				
	Sales Book B. p. 1 . .	140	00		
1	**3** *To Merchandise* . .			140	00
	——— // ———				
2	*Cash* Dr.	1060	00		
8	*Bills Receivable No. 1* . .	1000	00		
	In full of his Acct.				
4	**4** *To James Armitage* .			2060	00
	——— *Feb. 6th.* ———				
12	*Wagon Shop* Dr.				
	Cost of Shop and Lot 900.00				
	For Tools and Stock 400.00	1300	00		
2	*To Cash*			500	00
7	**5** // *Bills Payable No. 1*			800	00
		18608	00	18608	00

Tuesday, Feb. 7th, 1860. 2

(Pages 199 and 200.)

1	*Merchandise* *Dr.*				
	Invoice No. 1	*2750*	*00*		
10	*Expenses*				
	To New York for Goods 37.40				
	For Freight on do. 45.10	*82*	*50*		
2	*To Cash*			*582*	*50*
7	**6** *" Bills Payable No. 2*			*2250*	*00*
	Feb. 11th.				
10	*John Porter* *Dr.*	*860*	*00*		
2	*Cash*	*326*	*00*		
	Sales Book B. p. 8				
1	**7** *To Merchandise* . .			*1186*	*00*
	Feb. 13th.				
12	*Wagon Shop* *Dr.*				
	For Stock purchased . . .	*1775*	*60*		
7	*To Henry King* . .			*1550*	*00*
2	**8** *" Cash*			*225*	*60*
	Feb. 15th.				
11	*Stone Mill* *Dr.*				
	For 3 mos. Rent $300.00				
	" Sundry Fixtures 256.00	*556*	*00*		
2	**9** *To Cash*			*556*	*00*
	Feb. 16th.				
9	*Isaac Newton* *Dr.*				
	Sales Book B. p. 16 . .	*280*	*50*		
1	**10** *To Merchandise* . .			*280*	*50*
		6630	*60*	*6630*	*60*

Monday, February 20th, 1860.

(Page 200.)

		Dr.		Cr.	
11	Stone Mill Dr.				
	For 1860 Bu. Wheat @ 1.20	2232	00		
7	**11** To Bills Payable No. 3			2232	00
	Feb. 22d.				
10	John Porter Dr.				
	For 8 Cutters @ $45. 360.00				
	" 1 Buggy . . . 120.00	480	00		
12	**12** To Wagon Shop			480	00
	Feb. 24th.				
8	Ira Mayhew Dr.				
	For 1 Cutter	45	00		
5	Phineas Graves				
	For 1 Sleigh	50	00		
12	**13** To Wagon Shop . .			95	00
	Feb. 27th.				
1	Merchandise Dr.				
	Invoice No. 2	2800	00		
11	To Stone Mill				
	For 300 Bbls. Flour @ $6.			1800	00
12	To Wagon Shop				
	14 For 8 Buggies @ $125.00 .			1000	00
	Feb. 29th.				
11	Stone Mill Dr.				
	For 901 $\frac{1}{49}$ Bu. Wheat @ 98c. $883				
	" 650 " " @ 1.02 663	1546	00		
1	**15** To Merchandise . .			1546	00
		7153	00	7153	00

Thursday, March 1st, 1860.

(Page 201.)

7	Bills Payable No. 3 Dr.					
	For 20 L. Wagons @ $75.	1500				
	" 12 D. Sleighs @ 61.	732	2232	00		
12	**16** To Wagon Shop .				2232	00
	March 2d.					
2	Cash Dr.		1005	00		
8	To Bills Receivable No. 1				1000	00
6	**17** " Interest . . .				5	00
	March 6th.					
7	Bills Payable No. 1 Dr.					
	For 130 Bbls. Flour @ $6.	780				
	" 2 Tons Shorts @ 10.	20	800	00		
11	**18** To Stone Mill . .				800	00
	March 7th.					
4	John Hinman Dr.		1720	00		
	For 200 Bbls. Flour @ $6					
11	To Stone Mill . .				1200	00
	For 8 Lumber Wagons @ $65					
12	**19** To Wagon Shop				520	00
	March 9th.					
5	Clark & Smith Dr.		1710	00		
	For 12 Carriages @ $75. .					
12	To Wagon Shop . .				900	00
	For 85 Bbls. Flour @ $6.	510				
	" 20 Tons Ship Stuff @ 15.	300				
11	**20** To Stone Mill . .				810	00
			7467	00	7467	00

5 *Saturday, March 10th, 1860.*

(Pages 201 and 202.)

		Dr. $	cts.	Cr. $	cts.
11	*Stone Mill* Dr.				
	For 2700 Bu. Wheat @ $1. $2700				
	" 1900 Barrels @ 31 c. 589	3289	00		
12	*Wagon Shop*				
	For 1 mo. Wages of Foreman 50				
	" Stock, Invoice No. 3. 1270	1320	00		
2	**21** *To Cash . . . .*			4609	00
	March 12th.				
6	*Hill & Wright* Dr.	1825	00		
	For 250 Bbls. Flour @ $6				
11	*To Stone Mill . .*			1500	00
	For 5 Lumber Wagons @ $65				
12	**22** *To Wagon Shop .*			325	00
	March 14th.				
8	*Bills Receivable No. 2* Dr.	2595	00		
	Sales Book B. p. 40				
1	*To Merchandise . .*			2400	00
	For 3 Lumber Wagons @ $65				
12	**23** *To Wagon Shop . .*			195	00
	March 16th.				
9	*Isaac Newton* Dr.	250	00		
	For 1 Lumber Wagon				
12	*To Wagon Shop . .*			60	00
	For 20 Bbls. Flour @ $6.50 130				
	" 10 do. do. 6.00 60				
11	**24** *To Stone Mill . .*			190	00
		9279	00	9279	00

Monday, March 19th, 1860.

(Pages 202 and 203.)

12		Wagon Shop Dr.				
		For assorted Stock of Wood	652	50		
9		To Isaac Newton .			265	00
		For Invoice No. 4, Hardware				
6	**25**	To Hill & Wright .			387	50
		March 20th.				
1		Merchandise Dr.				
		Invoice No. 5	2944	00		
10		Expenses				
		To New York for Goods $24				
		For Freight on do. 27	51	00		
2	**26**	To Cash			2995	00
		March 22d.				
8		Ira Mayhew Dr.				
		For Order to H. King . .	65	00		
12	**27**	To Wagon Shop . .			65	00
		"				
10		Expenses Dr.				
		Clerk Hire $75				
		Fuel and Lights . . 30	105	00		
2	**28**	To Cash . . .			105	00
		March 24th.				
5		Phineas Graves Dr.				
		For his Order	135	60		
11		To Stone Mill . .			65	00
1	**29**	" Merchandise . .			70	60
			3953	10	3953	10

7 **Monday, March 26th, 1860.**

L.F.			Dr.		Cr.	
		(Page 203.)				
8		Bills Receivable No. 3				
		For 560 Bbls. Flour @ $6	3360	00		
11	**30**	To Stone Mill . .			3360	00
		—— // ——				
10		John Porter Dr.				
		Sales Book B. p. 60 . .	375	00		
1		To Merchandise . .			225	00
		For 25 Bbls. Flour @ $6 .				
11	**31**	To Stone Mill . .			150	00
		—— March 27th. ——				
2		Wagon Shop Dr.				
		For assorted Stock of Wood	552	00		
7		To Henry King . .			230	00
		For making 8 Buggies @ $19				
10		To John Porter . .			152	00
		For making 10 Sleighs @ 17				
9	**32**	To Isaac Newton .			170	00
		—— March 29th. ——				
8		Bills Receivable No. 4				
		In full of their Acct. . .	2790	00		
3	**33**	To S. C. Wood & Co.			2790	00
		—— March 30th. ——				
4		James Armitage Dr.				
		For 25 Bbls. Flour @ $6 150.00				
		" 2 Tons Shorts @ 10 20.00	170	00		
11	**34**	To Stone Mill . .			170	00
			7247	00	7247	00

Tuesday, April 3d, 1860. 8

(Page 205.)

			Dr.		Cr.	
7		Henry King Dr.				
		For his Draft to Wood & Co.	1275	00		
2		To Cash			125	00
		For 1 Carriage				
12		To Wagon Shop . .			225	00
3	35	" S. C. Wood & Co.			925	00
		April 5th.				
7		Henry King Dr.				
		For Order to Clark & Smith	125	00		
11		Stone Mill				
		For 325 Bu. Wheat @ 95 c.	308	75		
8		Bills Receivable No. 5				
		For Balance of their Acct. .	776	25		
5	36	To Clark & Smith .			1210	00
		April 6th.				
4		James Armitage Dr.				
		Sales Book B. p. 75 . .	2500	00		
1	37	To Merchandise . .			2500	00
		April 9th.				
4		John Hinman Dr.	1807	75		
		For 8 Lum. Wagons @ $65				
12		To Wagon Shop . .			520	00
		For 160 Bbls. Flour @ $6.				
11		To Stone Mill . .			960	00
		Sales Book D. p. 1				
1	38	To Merchandise . .			327	75
			6792	75	6792	75

9 Thursday, April 12th, 1860.

(Pages 205 and 206.)

8	Bills Receivable Dr.				
	Barns & King's Note No. 6	3000	00		
6	Interest	35	00		
12	Wagon Shop				
	Invoice of Lumber No. 6 .	254	60		
4	**39** To John Hinman .			3289	60
	April 14th.				
2	Cash Dr.	2610	14		
8	To Bills Receivable No. 2			2595	00
6	**40** Interest			15	14
	April 16th.				
1	Merchandise Dr.				
	Invoice No. 6	3400	00		
10	Expenses				
	To Boston for Goods $35.00				
	For Freight on do. 23.00	58	00		
7	To Bills Payable No. 4			2500	00
2	**41** " Cash			958	00
	April 20th.				
3	S. C. Wood & Co. Dr.	2325	50		
	Sales Book D. p. 10 . .				
1	To Merchandise . .			1125	50
	For 8 Buggies @ $105 . .				
12	To Wagon Shop . .			840	00
	For 60 Bbls. Flour @ $6				
11	**42** To Stone Mill . .			360	00
		11683	24	11683	24

Monday, April 23d, 1860. 10

(Pages 206 and 207.)

Fol.		Dr. $	cts.	Cr. $	cts.
2	Cash Dr.				
	For Bank Certificate . .	2500	00		
12	To Wagon Shop				
	For 1 Single Wagon . .			125	00
11	To Stone Mill				
	For 20 Bbls. Sup. Flour @ 6.50			130	00
4	**43** To James Armitage .			2245	00
	April 26th.				
2	Cash Dr.	500	00		
11	Stone Mill				
	For 800 Bu. Wheat @ 1.05 .	840	00		
3	**44** To S. C. Wood & Co.			1340	00
	May 1st.				
2	Cash Dr.	2831	85		
8	To Bills Receivable, No. 4			2790	00
6	**45** " Interest			41	85
	May 3d.				
4	James Armitage Dr.				
	Sales Book D. p. 25	1240	75		
1	**46** To Merchandise . .			1240	75
	"				
4	John Hinman Dr.	1550	00		
	Sales Book D. p. 30				
1	To Merchandise . .			1422	00
	For 20 Bbls. Flour @ $6.40				
11	**47** To Stone Mill . .			128	00
		9462	60	9462	60

Saturday, May 5th, 1860.

(Page 207.)

2	Cash Dr.				
	Clark & Smith's Note No. 5	776	25		
8	**48** To Bills Receivable .			776	25
	May 7th.				
7	Bills Payable Dr.				
	Our Note No. 2 to Hooker & Co.	2250	00		
6	" Interest	22	50		
2	**49** To Cash			2272	50
	May 8th.				
12	Wagon Shop Dr.				
	Invoice of Lumber No. 7 .	475	00		
5	Phineas Graves				
	For Order to Henry King .	125	00		
2	To Cash			75	00
7	**50** " Henry King . .			525	00
	May 10th.				
11	Stone Mill Dr.				
	For 603 Bu. Wheat @ $1.00	603	00		
8	Ira Mayhew				
	For Order to Isaac Newton	240	00		
9	Isaac Newton				
	For Balance of Purchase .	721	50		
12	To Wagon Shop				
	For 24 Lumber Wagons @ $60			1440	00
2	To Cash				
	51 On Ira Mayhew's Order			124	50
		5213	25	5213	25

Saturday, May 12th, 1860.

(Pages 207 and 208.)

4	James Armitage Dr.				
	For Accepted Order . . .	36	30		
9	Profit and Loss	24	20		
3	**52** To S. C. Wood & Co.			60	50
	May 15th.				
11	Stone Mill Dr.				
	For 3 months' Rent . .	300	00		
2	**53** To Cash			300	00
	May 18th.				
6	Hill & Wright Dr.	900	00		
	Sales Book D. p. 36				
1	To Merchandise . .			750	00
	For 25 Bbls. of Flour @ $6				
11	**54** To Stone Mill . .			150	00
	May 21st.				
2	Cash Dr.	3055	00		
	Barns & King's Note No. 6				
8	To Bills Receivable .			3000	00
6	**55** " Interest . . .			55	00
	May 23d.				
2	Cash Dr.	1905	00		
	Lease, Fixtures and Stock				
11	To Stone Mill . .			1680	00
	For 1 Carriage $185.00				
	" 1 Cutter 40.00				
12	**56** To Wagon Shop . .			225	00
		6220	50	6220	50

Saturday, May 26th, 1860.

(Pages 208 and 209.)

			Dr.		Cr.	
2		Cash Dr.				
		Note No. 3 of S. Rice	3399	20		
8		To Bills Receivable .			3360	00
6	57	" Interest . . .			39	20
		May 28th.				
12		Wagon Shop Dr.				
		For Labor and Stock . .	1062	30		
11		Stone Mill				
		For Labor and Stock . .	2203	25		
2	58	To Cash			3265	55
		May 29th.				
1		Merchandise Dr.				
		Invoice No. 8	2212	00		
10		Expenses				
		Freight and Insurance . .	32	62		
7		To Bills Payable				
		For our Note No. 5			1200	00
2	59	To Cash			1044	62
		May 30th.				
10		Expenses Dr.				
		In attending Fair . . .	45	50		
2		Cash				
		Premiums over Expenses . .	4	50		
9		To Profit and Loss				
	60	Prem. on Wagon $30				
		Prem. on Flour 20			50	00
			$959	37	$959	37

Thursday, May 31st, 1860.

(Page 209.)

	Sundries Dr.				
	In Am'ts to Balance				
1	Merchandise				
	Gross Profits in Trade . .	1224	62		
6	Interest	98	69		
11	Stone Mill	1575	00		
12	Wagon Shop	2755	00		
9	**61** To Profit & Loss .			5653	31
	——— // ———				
9	Profit & Loss Dr.				
	In Am't to Balance . .	374	62		
10	**62** To Expenses . . .			374	62
	——— // ———				
9	Profit & Loss Dr.				
	Net Gain in Business . .	5304	49		
3	**63** To Stock			5304	49
		11332	42	11332	42

NOTE. The last three entries above, are made for the purpose of closing the Ledger, as were the last three on page 191 of Book-keeping referred to in the Note at the foot of that page. These entries are referred to in Art. 306 of Book-keeping, (p. 182,) and are fully explained in that and the two preceding articles.

INDEX TO LEDGER B.—DOUBLE ENTRY.

(Pages 198 to 209.)

Dr. Merchandise Cr. 1

(Pages 198 to 209.)

1860.						1860.					
Feb.	1	To J.	1	1471	00	Feb.	2	By J.	1	140	00
"	7	"	2	2750	00	"	11	"	2	1186	00
"	27	"	3	2800	00	"	16	"	2	280	50
Mar.	20	"	6	2944	00	"	29	"	3	1546	00
						Mar.	14	"	5	2400	00
						"	24	"	6	70	60
						"	26	"	7	225	00
						"	30	Balance		4116	90
				9965	00					9965	00

Dr. Merchandise Cr.

1860.						1860.					
Apr.	2	Bal.		4116	90	Apr.	6	By J.	8	2500	00
"	16	To J.	9	3400	00	"	9	"	8	327	75
May	29	"	13	2212	00	"	20	"	9	1125	50
"	31	"	14	1224	62	May	3	"	10	1240	75
						"	3	"	10	1422	00
						"	18	"	12	750	00
						"	31	Invt.		3587	52
				10953	52					10953	52
June	1	Inv.		3587	52						

2 Dr. **Cash** Cr.

(Pages 198 to 209.)

1860.						1860.					
Feb.	1	To J.	1	7812	00	Feb.	6	By J.	1	500	00
"	2	"	1	1060	00	"	7	"	2	582	50
"	11	"	2	326	00	"	13	"	2	225	60
Mar.	2	"	4	1005	00	"	15	"	2	556	00
						Mar.	10	"	5	4609	00
						"	20	"	6	2995	00
						"	22	"	6	105	00
						"	30	Balance		629	90
				10203	00					10203	00

Dr. **Cash** Cr.

1860.						1860.					
Apr.	2	Bal.		629	90	Apr.	3	By J.	8	125	00
"	14	To J.	9	2610	14	"	16	"	9	958	00
"	23	"	10	2500	00	May	7	"	11	2272	50
"	26	"	10	500	00	"	8	"	11	75	00
May	1	"	10	2831	85	"	10	"	11	124	50
"	5	"	11	776	25	"	15	"	12	300	00
"	21	"	12	3055	00	"	28	"	13	3265	55
"	23	"	12	1905	00	"	29	"	13	1044	62
"	26	"	13	3399	20	"	31	Balance		10046	67
"	30	"	13	4	50						
				18211	84					18211	84
June	1	Bal.		10046	67						

Dr. S. C. Wood & Co. Cr.

(Pages 198 to 209.)

1860.						1860.					
Feb.	1	To J.	1	2650	00	Mar.	29	By J.	7	2790	00
"	1	"	1	140	00						
				2790	00					2790	00
Apr.	20	To J.	9	2325	50	Apr.	3	By J.	8	925	00
						"	26	"	10	1340	00
						"	12	"	12	60	50
				2325	50					2325	50

Dr. Stock Cr.

1860.						1860.					
Feb.	1	To J.	1	1115	00	Feb.	1	By J.	1	13993	00
Mar.	30	Balance		12878	00						
				13993	00					13993	00
May	31	Balance		18182	49	Apr.	2	Bal.		12878	00
						May	31	By J.	14	5304	49
				18182	49					18182	49
						June	1	Bal.		18182	49

8 85

4 Dr. James Armitage Cr.

(Pages 198 to 209.)

1860.						1860.					
Feb.	1	To J.	1	2060	00	Feb.	2	By J.	1	2060	00
Mar.	30	"	7	170	00	Apr.	23	"	10	2245	00
Apr.	6	"	8	2500	00	May	31	Balance		1702	05
May	3	"	10	1240	75						
"	12	"	12	36	30						
				6007	05					6007	05
June	1	Bal.		1702	05						

Dr. John Hinman Cr.

1860.						1860.					
Mar.	7	To J.	4	1720	00	Apr.	12	By J.	9	3289	60
Apr.	9	"	8	1807	75	May	31	Balance		1788	15
May	3	"	10	1550	00						
				5077	75					5077	75
June	1	Bal.		1788	15						

Dr. Clark & Smith Cr. 5

(Pages 198 to 209.)

1860.						1860.					
Mar.	9	To J.	4	1710	00	Feb.	1	By J.	1	500	00
						Mar.	30	Balance		1210	00
				1710	00					1710	00
Apr.	2	Bal.		1210	00	Apr.	5	By J.	8	1210	00

Dr. Phineas Graves Cr.

1860.						1860.					
Feb.	24	To J.	3	50	00	Mar.	30	Balance		185	60
Mar.	24	"	6	135	60						
				185	60					185	60
Apr.	2	Bal.		185	60	May	31	Balance		310	60
May	8	To J.	11	125	00						
				310	60					310	60
June	1	Bal.		310	60						

6 Dr. Hill & Wright Cr.

(Pages 198 to 209.)

1860.						1860.					
Mar.	12	To J.	5	1825	00	Feb.	1	By J.	1	615	00
						Mar.	19	"	6	387	50
						"	30	Balance		822	50
				1825	00					1825	00
Apr.	2	Bal.		822	50	May	31	Balance		1722	50
May	18		12	900	00						
				1722	50					1722	50
June	1	Bal.		1722	50						

Dr. Interest Cr.

1860.						1860.					
Apr.	12	To J.	9	35	00	Mar.	2	By J.	4	5	00
May	7	"	11	22	50	Apr.	14	"	9	15	14
"	31	"	14	98	69	May	1	"	10	41	85
						"	21	"	12	55	00
						"	26	"	13	39	20
				156	19					156	19

Dr. Bills Payable Cr. 7

(Pages 198 to 209.)

1860.						1860.					
Mar.	1	No. 3	4	2232	00	Feb.	6	No. 1	1	800	00
"	6	" 1	4	800	00	"	7	" 2	2	2250	00
"	30	Balance		2250	00	"	20	" 3	3	2232	00
				5282	00					5282	00
May	7	No. 2	11	2250	00	Apr.	2	Bal.		2250	00
"	31	Balance		3700	00	"	16	No. 4	9	2500	00
						May	29	" 5	13	1200	00
				5950	00					5950	00
						June	1	Bal.		3700	00

Dr. Henry King Cr.

1860.						1860.					
Mar.	30	Balance		1780	00	Feb.	13	By J.	2	1550	00
						Mar.	27	"	7	230	00
				1780	00					1780	00
Apr.	3	To J.	8	1275	00	Apr.	2	Bal.		1780	00
"	5	"	8	125	00	May	8	By J.	11	525	00
May	31	Balance		905	00						
				2305	00					2305	00
						June	1	Bal.		905	00

8 Dr. **Bills Receivable** Cr.

(Pages 198 to 209.)

1860.						1860.					
Feb.	2	No. 1	1	1000	00	Mar.	2	No. 1	4	1000	00
Mar.	14	" 2	5	2595	00	"	30	Balance		8745	00
"	26	" 3	7	3360	00						
"	29	" 4	7	2790	00						
				9745	00					9745	00
Apr.	2	Bal.		8745	00	Apr.	14	No. 2	9	2595	00
"	5	No. 5	8	776	25	May	1	" 4	10	2790	00
"	12	" 6	9	3000	00	"	5	" 5	11	776	25
						"	21	" 6	12	3000	00
						"	26	" 3	13	3360	00
				12521	25					12521	25

Dr. **Ira Mayhew** Cr.

1860.						1860.					
Feb.	24	To J.	3	45	00	Mar.	30	Balance		110	00
Mar.	22	"	6	65	00						
				110	00					110	00
Apr.	2	Bal.		110	00	May	31	Balance		350	00
May	10	To J.	11	240	00						
				350	00					350	00
June	1	Bal.		350	00						

Dr. Profit & Loss Cr. 9

(Pages 198 to 209.)

1860.						1860.					
May	12	To J.	12	24	20	May	30	By J.	13	50	00
"	31	"	14	374	62	"	31	"	14	5653	31
"	31	"	14	5304	49						
				5703	31					5703	31

Dr. Isaac Newton Cr.

1860.						1860.					
Feb.	16	To J.	2	280	50	Mar.	19	By J.	6	265	00
Mar.	16	"	5	250	00	"	27	"	7	170	00
						"	30	Balance		95	50
				530	50					530	50
Apr.	2	Bal.		95	50	May	31	Balance		817	00
May	10	To J.	11	721	50						
				817	00					817	00
June	1	Bal.		817	00						

10 Dr. **Expenses** Cr.

(Pages 198 to 209.)

1860.						1860.					
Feb.	7	To J.	2	82	50	Mar.	30	Balance		238	50
Mar.	20	"	6	51	00						
"	22	"	6	105	00						
				238	50					238	50
Apl.	2	Bal.		238	50	May	31	By J.	14	374	62
"	16	To J.	9	58	00						
May	29	"	13	32	62						
"	30	"	13	45	50						
				374	62					374	62

Dr. **John Porter** Cr.

1860.						1860.					
Feb.	11	To J.	2	860	00	Mar.	27	By J.	7	152	00
"	22	"	3	480	00	"	30	Balance		1563	00
Mar.	26	"	7	375	00						
				1715	00					1715	00
Apr.	2	Bal.		1563	00						

Dr. Stone Mill Cr. 11

(Pages 198 to 209.)

1860.						1860.					
Feb.	15	To J.	2	556	00	Feb.	27	By J.	3	1800	00
"	20	"	3	2232	00	Mar.	6	"	4	800	00
"	29	"	3	1546	00	"	7	"	4	1200	00
Mar.	10	"	5	3289	00	"	9	"	4	810	00
"	30	Balance		2422	00	"	12	"	5	1500	00
						"	16	"	5	190	00
						"	24	"	6	65	00
						"	26	"	7	3360	00
						"	26	"	7	150	00
						"	30	"	7	170	00
				10045	00					10045	00

Dr. Stone Mill Cr.

1860.						1860.					
Apr.	5	To J.	8	308	75	Apr.	2	Bal.		2422	00
"	26	"	10	840	00	"	9	By J.	8	960	00
May	10	"	11	603	00	"	20	"	9	360	00
"	15	"	12	300	00	"	23	"	10	130	00
"	28	"	13	2203	25	May	3	"	10	128	00
"	31	"	14	1575	00	"	18	"	12	150	00
						"	23	"	12	1680	00
				5830	00					5830	00

12 **Dr.** Wagon Shop **Cr.**

(Pages 198 to 209.)

1860.						1860.					
Feb.	6	To J.	1	1300	00	Feb.	22	By J.	3	480	00
"	13	"	2	1775	60	"	24	"	3	95	00
Mar.	10	"	5	1320	00	"	27	"	3	1000	00
"	19	"	6	652	50	Mar.	1	"	4	2232	00
"	27	"	7	552	00	"	7	"	4	520	00
"	30	Balance		271	90	"	9	"	4	900	00
						"	12	"	5	325	00
						"	14	"	5	195	00
						"	16	"	5	60	00
						"	22	"	6	65	00
				5872	00					5872	00

Dr. Wagon Shop **Cr.**

1860.						1860.					
Apr.	12	To J.	9	254	60	Apr.	2	Bal.		271	90
May	8	"	11	475	00	"	3	By J.	8	225	00
"	28	"	13	1062	30	"	9	"	8	520	00
"	31	"	14	2755	00	"	20	"	9	840	00
						"	23	"	10	125	00
						May	10	"	11	1440	00
						"	23	"	12	225	00
						"	31	Invt.		900	00
				4546	90					4546	90
June	1	Invt.		900	00						

TRIAL BALANCE.

(Pages 198 to 213.)

Ans. 1st.

Dr.	Balances of May 30th, 1860.				Cr.
Merchandise, p. 1	2362	90	Stock, p. 3	12878	00
Cash, p. 2	10046	67	Interest, p. 6	98	69
Jas. Armitage, 4	1702	05	Bills Payable, p. 7	3700	00
John Hinman, 4	1788	15	Henry King, p. 7	905	00
Phineas Graves, 5	310	60	Profit & Loss, p. 9	25	80
Hill & Wright, 6	1722	50	Stone Mill, p. 11	1575	00
Ira Mayhew, p. 8	350	00	Wagon Shop, 12	1855	00
Isaac Newton, 9	817	00			
Expenses, p. 10	374	62			
John Porter, p. 10	1563	00			
	21037	49		21037	49

LEDGER BALANCES.

Ans. 2d.

Dr.	June 1st, 1860.				Cr.
Merchandise, p. 1	3587	52	Stock, p. 3	18182	49
Cash, p. 2	10046	67	Bills Payable, p. 7	3700	00
Jas. Armitage, 4	1702	05	Henry King, p. 7	905	00
John Hinman, 4	1788	15			
Phineas Graves, 5	310	60			
Hill & Wright, 6	1722	50			
Ira Mayhew, 8	350	00			
Isaac Newton, 9	817	00			
John Porter, p. 10	1563	00			
Wagon Shop, 12	900	00			
	22787	49		22787	49

(Pages 198 to 213.)

Ans. 3d. The Dr. Ledger Balances on the preceding page constitute our *Assets,* and consist of Merchandise, Cash, Wagon Shop, and Personal Accounts.

Ans. 4th. The Cr. Ledger Balances on the preceding page, except Stock, are our *Liabilities,* and consist of Bills Payable, and a Personal Account we owe Henry King.

Ans. 5th. *The Net value of our Stock,* including the indebtedness of both Partners to the Firm, is $18182.49.

Ans. 6th. Net value of Ira Mayhew's Stock, after paying his personal indebtedness to the Firm, $10180.245.

Net value of Phineas Graves' Stock, after paying his personal indebtedness to the Firm, $7341.645.

Calculation for Ira Mayhew's Net Stock.

Net Value of our Stock June 1st, ...	$18182.49
Net value of our Stock Feb. 1st, ...	12878.00
Net Gain to be divided equally, ...	$5304.49
Net Gain of each Partner, ...	$2652.245
Stock put in by Ira Mayhew Feb. 1st, . . .	7878.00
Ira Mayhew's Assets June 1st, ...	$10530.245
Deduct his personal indebtedness of	350.00
Ira Mayhew's *Net Stock* is	$10180.245

Calculation for Phineas Graves' Net Stock.

Stock put in by Phineas Graves Feb. 1st, . .	$5000.00
Net Gain of each Partner, ...	2652.245
Phineas Graves' Assets June 1st, ...	$7652.245
Deduct his personal indebtedness of	310.60
Phineas Graves' *Net Stock* is	$7341.645

ILLUSTRATIVE EXAMPLE.

FIFTH FORM OF ACCOUNTS.

(Pages 214 to 218.)

The following are my Assets and Liabilities at the time of opening the Journal of the Illustrative Example in the Book-keeping, Fifth Form of Accounts, pages 216 and 217, and the Transactions upon which it is based.

MY ASSETS. *May* 1*st*, 1860.

I have Merchandise in Store worth as per Inventory, $2700.00; Cash in Safe and Bank to the amount of $475.00; Bills Receivable No. 1, being a Note against J. Brooks for $275.00, as per Bill Book; and John Cook owes me a balance on account of $350.00.

MY LIABILITIES.

I owe John Hill $230.00 on account, and I owe on Bills Payable No. 1, as per Bill Book, $220.00.

Friday, May 4*th*, 1860.

Transaction 1. John Hill has bought Merchandise of me on account, as follows: 20 lbs. of Sugar at 9 c. a lb.; 9 yds. of Black Cloth at $4.50 a yard; and 2 Boxes of Raisins at $3.00 a box.

Saturday, May 5*th*, 1860.

Tr. 2. I have sold $125.00 worth of Merchandise this week for Cash, as per Cash Book, which I enter in the Journal.

Tuesday, May 8*th*, 1860.

Tr. 3. Wm. Cook has bought of me on account, 14 lbs. of Putty at 8 c. a lb.; 12 yds. of Black Silk at 90 c. a yard; and 44 yds. of Cotton Cloth at 9 c. a yard.

(Page 214 to 218.)

Thursday, May 10th, 1860.

Tr. 4. H. Allen has made repairs on my Store to the amount of $15.50, as per Bill rendered, for which I charge Store Expenses and credit him in account.

Saturday, May 12th, 1860.

Tr. 5. Cash sales of Merchandise this week have been $200.00, as per Cash Book, which I carry to the Journal.

Monday, May 14th, 1860.

Tr. 6. A son of John Hill has brought an Order from his Father for Merchandise, on which I have paid $24.35, as per Bill rendered.

Thursday, May 17th, 1860.

Tr. 7. I have sold Merchandise to John Cook on account, as follows: 26 yds. of Sheeting at 25 c. a yard; 12 yds. of Blue Silk at 75 c. a yard; and 18 lbs. of Crushed Sugar at 9 c. a lb.

Saturday, May 19th, 1860.

Tr. 8. I have sent $22.15 worth of Merchandise to the house, and furnished $10.00 in money for Family Expenses.

Tr. 9. Cash sales of Merchandise this week have been $227.60, as per Cash Book.

Monday, May 21st, 1860.

Tr. 10. Ira Graves has brought an Order on me from Wm. Cook for $52.00 worth of Merchandise. Graves receives $32.00 of this amount in goods, and the balance of the Order is placed to his credit in account.

Saturday, May 26th, 1860.

Tr. 11. Cash sales of Merchandise this week have amounted to $225.50, as per Cash Book.

(Pages 214 to 218.)

Monday, May 28th, 1860.

Tr. 12. I have sold 10 lbs. of Crushed Sugar at 9 c. a lb., and 4 yds. of Cassimere at $2.50 a yard, to Ira Graves, and charged him for the same in account.

Wednesday, May 30th, 1860.

Tr. 13. I have paid $8.00 in Cash for a Chandelier for the Store, and charged the same to Store Expenses.

Thursday, May 31st, 1860.

Tr. 14. I have sold to Ira Graves 8 yds. of Cambric at 9 c. a yard, and 10 yds. of Gingham at 31 c. a yard. It being the close of the Month, I post to the credit Merchandise the amount sold during the month.

Remark. In writing out the Transactions of this Illustrative Example, in accordance with the directions of Art. 320 of Book-keeping, (p. 215,) should the learner fail to employ the precise language here used, it matters not, so long as the *ideas* are the same as those here given. The language employed by different persons in writing these Transactions may be various, and yet all may be equally correct. This translation of Journal Entry to Transaction thus becomes at once the gymnastics of Book-keeping, and a valuable exercise in Composition.

INDEX TO LEDGER C.—DOUBLE ENTRY.

(Pages 216 to 218.)

Dr. Merchandise Cr. 1

(Pages 216 to 218.)

1860.						1860.					
May	1	To J.	1	2700	00	May	31	By J.	2	952	62
"	31	Bal.	3	412	62	"	31	Invt.		2160	00
				3112	62					3112	62
June	1			2160	00						

Dr. Cash Cr.

1860.						1860.					
May	1	To J.	1	475	00	May	19	By J.	2	10	00
"	5	"	1	125	00	"	30	"	2	8	00
"	12	"	1	200	00	"	31	Balance		1235	10
"	19	"	2	227	60						
"	26	"	2	225	50						
				1253	10					1253	10
June	1	Bal.		1235	10						

2 Dr. **Bills Receivable** Cr.

(Pages 216 to 218.)

1860.										
May	1	No. 1	1	275	00					

Dr. **Stock** Cr.

1860.						1860.					
May	1	To J.	1	450	00	May	1	By J.	1	3800	00
"	31	Balance		3706	97	"	31	P. & L.	3	356	97
				4156	97					4156	97
						June	1	Bal.		3706	97

Dr. **John Cook** Cr.

1860.						1860.					
May	1	To J.	1	350	00	May	31	Balance		367	12
"	17	"	2	17	12						
				367	12					367	12
June	1	Bal.		367	12						

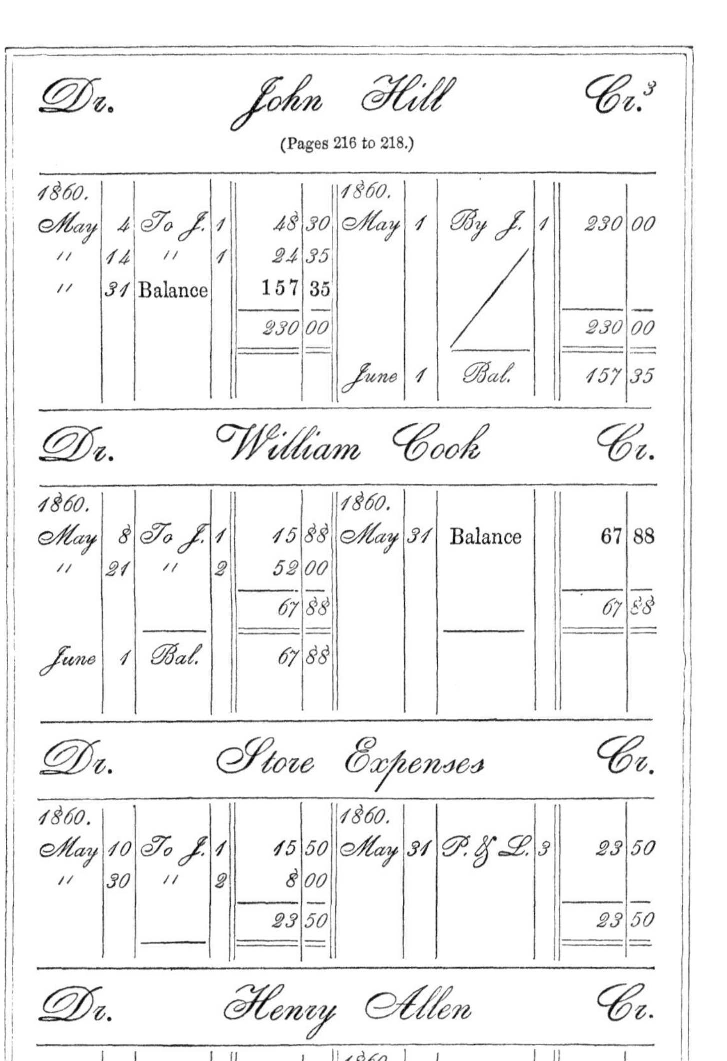

Dr. John Hill Cr. 3

(Pages 216 to 218.)

1860.				$	cts.	1860.				$	cts.
May	4	To J.	1	48	30	May	1	By J.	1	230	00
"	14	"	1	24	35						
"	31	Balance		157	35						
				230	00					230	00
						June	1	Bal.		157	35

Dr. William Cook Cr.

1860.				$	cts.	1860.				$	cts.
May	8	To J.	1	15	88	May	31	Balance		67	88
"	21	"	2	52	00						
				67	88					67	88
June	1	Bal.		67	88						

Dr. Store Expenses Cr.

1860.				$	cts.	1860.				$	cts.
May	10	To J.	1	15	50	May	31	P. & L.	3	23	50
"	30	"	2	8	00						
				23	50					23	50

Dr. Henry Allen Cr.

				$	cts.	1860.				$	cts.
						May	10	By J.	1	15	50

4

Dr. Family Expenses Cr.

(Pages 216 to 218.)

Date				$	¢	Date				$	¢
1860.						1860.					
May	19	To J.	2	32	15	May	31	P. & L.	3	32	15

Dr. Bills Payable Cr.

Date				$	¢	Date				$	¢
						1860.					
						May	1	No. 1	1	220	00

Dr. Ira Graves Cr.

Date				$	¢	Date				$	¢
1860.						1860.					
May	28	To J.	2	10	90	May	21	By J.	2	20	00
"	31	"	2	3	82						
"	31	Balance		5	28						
				20	00					20	00
						June	1	Bal.		5	28

Dr. Profit & Loss Cr.

Date				$	¢	Date				$	¢
1860.						1860.					
May	31	Exs.	3	55	65	May	31	Mdse.	3	412	62
"	31	Stock	3	356	97						
				412	62					412	62

Boston, Tuesday, May 31st, 1860. 3

(Pages 216 to 218.)

L. F.		Sund's	Dr.	Sund's	Cr.	Mdse.	Cr.
1	Merchandise Dr.						
	Gross Profits in Trade .	412	62				
4	To Profit & Loss .			412	62		
	"						
4	Profit & Loss Dr.						
	In Amounts to Balance .	55	65				
3	To Store Expenses .			23	50		
4	" Family Expenses			32	15		
	"						
4	Profit & Loss Dr.						
	Net Profit in Trade . .	356	97				
2	To Stock			356	97		
		825	24	825	24		

Above are the closing entries and 3d page of the Journal of the Illustrative Example, Fifth Form of Accounts. The Journal, as given in the Book-keeping, pages 216 and 217, when posted to the Ledger will give, under date of May 31st, 1860, the Trial Balance that appears on page 218 of Book-keeping. The Merchandise on hand May 31st, is worth \$2160.00, as per Inventory, (Art. 320, p. 215 of Book-keeping.) This sum being entered to the credit of Merchandise, in the Ledger, we are prepared to close Mdse. into Profit and Loss, which is done by the first entry above. Profit and Loss is then made to close Store Expenses and Family Expenses, when it is itself closed into Stock. Then, by entering the Balances under date of May 31st, and bringing them down, we have the Ledger Balances of June 1st, 1860, with the *Net Gain* in business as indicated in the last Journal entry, to wit: \$356.97.

ILLUSTRATIVE EXAMPLE.

SIXTH FORM OF ACCOUNTS.

(Pages 219 to 223.)

The following are my Assets and Liabilities at the time of opening the Journal of the Illustrative Example in the Book-keeping, Sixth Form of Accounts, pp. 221 and 222, and the Transactions on which the Example is based.

My Assets. *June 1st*, 1860.

I have $2500.00 Cash in my safe, and $3400.00 Cash credit in the Mercantile Bank; there are owing to me on Bills Receivable, as per Bill Book, $2750.00; and S. Wood owes me $450.00 on account.

My Liabilities.

I owe on Personal Accounts to depositors, as follows: to Job Otis $360.00; to H. Smith $640.00; and to R. Cook $600.00.

Saturday, June 2d, 1860.

Transaction 1. O. Rood deposits with me $255.00 in Cash.

Tr. 2. Job Otis, a depositor, purchases of me a Draft on the Mercantile Bank for $375.00, for which I charge him in acct., Exchange being at a premium of 1 per cent.

Tr. 3. O. Rood deposits with me $560.00 in Cash.

Tr. 4. I sell to a customer a Draft on the Mercantile Bank for $250.00, Exchange being at a premium of 1 per cent., and receive payment therefor in Cash.

Tr. 5. I loan to a customer $350.00 on his Note No. 4, as per Bill Book, where particulars are stated.

Tr. 6. I remit $2000.00 to the Mercantile Bank to be placed to my credit in acct. (Charges for carriage are paid quarterly, and are not taken into the account here.)

(Pages 219 to 222.)

It being the close of the day I make up my Cash acct. The *footings* of the Cash columns and the *Balance* are entered as directed in Art. 322 of Book-keeping.

Monday, June 4th, 1860.

Tr. 7. S. Wood deposits with me $500.00 in Cash.

Tr. 8. Job Otis deposits with me $475.00 in Cash.

Tr. 9. H. Smith, a depositor, purchases of me a Draft on the Mercantile Bank for $400.00, which I charge to him in acct., Exchange being at a premium of 1 per cent.

Tr. 10. S. Wood deposits with me $360.00 in Cash.

Tr. 11. H. Smith deposits with me $275.00 in Cash.

Tr. 12. S. Wood procures of me a Draft on the Mercantile Bank for $475.00, which I charge to him in acct., Exchange being at a premium of 1 per cent.

Tr. 13. R. Cook deposits $247.50 in current funds.

Tr. 14. Bill Receivable No. 3, as per Bill Book, is this day taken up. The *face* of the Note is $276.00, and the Interest amounts to $3.75, both of which amounts are paid in Cash.

Tr. 15. I sell a Draft of $460.00 on the Mercantile Bank, for which I charge a premium of $1\frac{1}{2}$ per cent., payment being made in Western money which is at a discount.

Tr. 16. I loan to a customer $375.50 for which I receive his Note No. 5, as per Bill Book.

Tr. 17. I pay $127.20 on S. Wood's Check.

It being the close of the day, I make up my cash acct. As the Journal entries of the day were begun on one page, and continued on another, it becomes necessary in obtaining the amount of Cash received and paid out during the day, to consult both pages of the Journal on which the account has been entered.

(Pages 219 to 222.)

Thursday, June 5th, 1860.

Tr. 18. Bill Receivable No. 2, as per Bill Book, has this day been taken up. The Note which was given for $2290.00, has earned $80.00 Interest, all of which is paid in Cash.

Tr. 19. I remit to the Mercantile Bank $2500.00 for my credit in account.

Tr. 20. Job Otis deposits with me $384.00 in Cash.

Tr. 21. O. Rood deposits with me $265.88 in Cash.

Tr. 22. O. Rood procures a Draft on Mercantile Bank for $457.00, Exchange being at a premium of 1 per cent.

Tr. 23. S. Wood brings in $300.00 in Cash, and obtains a Draft on the Mercantile Bank for $175.00, for which I charge him a premium of 1 per cent. The balance of the $300.00 I enter to his credit in account.

Remark. The remark made at the 99th page of the Key is alike applicable to the precise language to be employed in the writing out of the preceding Transactions, and need not be repeated here.

In an account extending through any considerable length of time, there would of necessity be Dr. entries to Expenses, Exchange, and perhaps to Interest, which do not here appear. This omission accounts for but two Journal entries being required in closing the Ledger, instead of three, which in most cases are necessary, as is fully explained in Art. 305 of Book-keeping, (p. 182,) and which is exemplified in the closing Journal entries for the Fifth Form, at the 105th page of the Key.

INDEX TO LEDGER D.—DOUBLE ENTRY.

(Pages 221 to 223.)

A B		**M**	
Bills Receivable	2	*Mercantile Bank*	1
C		**N O**	
Cook, R.	4	*Otis, Job*	4
D		**P**	
		Profit & Loss	5
E		**Q R**	
Exchange	3	*Rood, O.*	3
F G H		**S**	
		Smith, H.	5
		Stock	1
I		**V W**	
Interest	5	*Wood, S.*	2
J K L		**X Y Z**	

1

Dr. Stock Cr.

(Pages 221 to 223.)

1860.						1860.					
June	1	To J.	1	1600	00	June	1	By J.	1	9100	00
"	7	Balance		7611	97	"	6	P. & L.	3	111	97
				9211	97					9211	97
						June	7	Bal.		7611	97

Dr. Mercantile Bank Cr.

1860.						1860.					
June	1	To J.	1	3400	00	June	2	By J.	1	375	00
"	2	"	1	2000	00	"	2	"	1	250	00
"	5	"	2	2500	00	"	4	"	1	400	00
						"	4	"	2	475	00
						"	4	"	2	460	00
						"	5	"	2	457	00
						"	5	"	2	175	00
						"	7	Balance		5308	00
				7900	00					7900	00
June	7	Bal.		5308	00						

Dr. Bills Receivable Cr.[2]

(Pages 221 to 223.)

1860.						1860.					
June	1	To J.	1	2750	00	June	4	By J.	2	276	00
"	2	"	1	350	00	"	5	"	2	2290	00
"	4	"	2	375	50	"	7	Balance		909	50
				3475	50					3475	50
June	7	Bal.		909	50						

Dr. S. Wood Cr.

1860.						1860.					
June	1	To J.	1	450	00	June	4	By J.	1	500	00
"	4	"	2	479	75	"	4	"	2	360	00
"	4	"	2	127	20	"	5	"	2	123	25
						"	7	Balance		73	70
				1056	95					1056	95
June	7	Bal.		73	70						

3 Dr. **Exchange** Cr.

(Pages 221 to 223.)

1860.						1860.					
June	6	P. & L.	3	28	22	June	2	By J.	1	3	75
						"	2	"	1	2	50
						"	4	"	1	4	00
						"	4	"	2	4	75
						"	4	"	2	6	90
						"	5	"	2	4	57
						"	5	"	2	1	75
				28	22					28	22

Dr. **O. Rood** Cr.

1860.						1860.					
June	5	To J.	2	461	57	June	2	By J.	1	255	00
"	7	Balance		619	31	"	2	"	1	560	00
						"	5	"	2	265	88
				1080	88					1080	88
						June	7	Bal.		619	31

Dr. **Job Otis** Cr. 4

(Pages 221 to 223.)

1860.						1860.					
June	2	To J.	1	378	75	June	1	By J.	1	360	00
"	7	Balance		840	25	"	4	"	1	475	00
						"	5	"	2	384	00
				1219	00					1219	00
						June	7	Bal.		840	25

Dr. **R. Cook** Cr.

1860.						1860.					
June	7	Balance		847	50	June	1	By J.	1	600	00
						"	4	"	2	247	50
				847	50					847	50
						June	7	Bal.		847	50

Dr. H. Smith Cr.

(Pages 221 to 223.)

1860.						1860.					
June	4	To J.	1	404	00	June	1	By J.	1	640	00
"	7	Balance		511	00	"	4	"	2	275	00
				915	00					915	00
						June	7	Bal.		511	00

Dr. Interest Cr.

1860.						1860.					
June	6	P. & L.	3	83	75	June	4	By J.	2	3	75
						"	5	"	2	80	00
				83	75					83	75

Dr. Profit & Loss Cr.

1860.						1860.					
June	6	Stock	3	111	97	June	6	By J.	3	111	97

Detroit, June 6th, 1860.

(Pages 221 to 223.)

Cash	Dr.	Sund's	Dr.	L. F.		Sund's	Cr.	Cash	Cr.
		28	22	3	Exchange				
		83	75	5	Interest				
				5	To Profit & Loss	111	97		
					"				
		111	97	5	Profit & Loss				
					Net Gain in bus.				
				1	To Stock . .	111	97		
		223	94		*Proof.*	223	94		

Above are the closing entries and 3d page of the Illustrative Example, Sixth Form of Accounts. The Journal, as given in the Book-keeping, pp. 221 and 222, when posted to the Ledger, will give the Trial Balance on page 223, with the exception of Cash; and the making up of the Cash Account for June 5th (p. 222) would show the amount of Cash to be $4138.83, as there stated.

For the purpose of rendering the closing entries more distinct, they are made under date of June 6th, so as to be readily noted when posted to the Ledger. The Ledger Balances are brought down under date of June 7th, for a like reason.

The second of the three closing entries referred to in Art. 305 of Book-keeping, (p. 182,) is wanting here. Two Journal entries are hence all that are required in closing this Ledger. When these are posted there will appear the Ledger Balances of June 7th, 1860. The last entry shows the *Net Gain* in business, to wit: $111.97.

OPENING JOURNAL ENTRIES.

EXAMPLE I.

(Pages 224 to 227.)

		Dr.		Cr.	
Sundries Dr.					
Merchandise		*22611*	*60*		
100 Bbls. Sugar, 200 lbs. @ 5¾ c.	*1150.*				
5 Hhds. Molas. 63 Gals. @ 27⅓ c.	*86.10*				
Sundries per Inventory	*21375.50*				
Bills Receivable		*3200*			
H. Paywell's Acceptance	*2000.*				
O. H. Bradbury's Note	*1200.*				
Cash		*1500*			
To Stock				*27311*	*60*
— // —					
Stock Dr.		*2231*	*12*		
To Bills Payable				*1975*	*37*
My Acceptance, J. Hunter	*475.37*				
My Note favor J. O. Baker	*1500.*				
To B. Howard Acct.				*255*	*75*

Total amount of my Assets, ...	$27311.60
" " " Liabilities, . .	2231.12
Net Stock on commencing business, . .	25080.48

NOTE. In the above Journal entries the amounts to be posted are entered *opposite* the Titles of Accounts to which they are to be posted, which some prefer to entering them *after the explanation.*

CLOSING JOURNAL ENTRIES.

EXAMPLE II.

(Pages 226 and 227.)

Having entered to the Cr. of Merchandise and Real Estate accounts the value of the amount on hand, per Inventory, we proceed to close the Ledger Accounts according to the directions of the Book-keeping. (Arts. 298 to 307.)

Sundries	Dr.				
Merchandise	Gross Profits	10623	25		
Interest	Gain on	260	60		
Discount	Gain on	825	50		
To Profit & Loss				11709	35
—— // ——					
Profit & Loss	Dr.	2070	58		
To Real Estate	Loss on			460	
" Expenses	Amount of			1526	30
" Exchange	Loss on			84	28
—— // ——					
Profit & Loss	Net Gain Dr.	9919	52		
To Stock				9919	52

EXPLANATION. These entries being posted as the work progresses, there will first be *eliminated* from the Ledger the Interest and Discount accounts; next, Expenses and Exchange; and finally, Profit and Loss. Merchandise and Real Estate accounts will be so *modified* as to show the value of what is on hand belonging to each; what has been *gained* on one, and what has been *lost* on the other, having been carried to Profit and Loss; while the Stock account, in its changed condition, will indicate the result of all the other changes taken together.

OPENING JOURNAL ENTRIES.

EXAMPLE III.

(Pages 227 and 228.)

Sundries Dr.				
Cash	3750	60		
Bills Receivable	3450	10		
H. K. Powers' Acct.	573			
Merchandise	11376	80		
To Ira Mayhew			19150	50
—— // ——				
Ira Mayhew Dr.	6150	50		
To Bills Payable			3600	
" Homer Brown			1460	50
" James Hill			1090	
—— // ——				
Sundries Dr.				
Cash	12500			
Merchandise	5500			
To H. Boomer			18000	

Or the two Opening Journal Entries for Ira Mayhew and the one for Hiram Boomer may be combined so as to form but one Opening Journal Entry, as presented on the next page of the Key, which gives the same result in a more compact form. These two methods are alike in good usage, and the book-keeper may safely adopt that which seems to him preferable.

OPENING JOURNAL ENTRY.

EXAMPLE III.

(Pages 227 and 228.)

Sundries *To Sundries*				
Cash Ira Mayhew, $ 3750.00 / H. Boomer, 12500.00	16250	60		
Bills Receivable	3450	10		
H. K. Powers' Acct.	573			
Merchandise Mayhew, $11376.80 / Boomer, 5500.00	16876	80		
To Ira Mayhew			13000	
" *Hiram Boomer*			18000	
" *Bills Payable*			3600	
" *Homer Brown*			1460	50
" *James Hill*			1090	

Ira Mayhew's Stock (Art. 330, Book-keeping) was	$35000
Less value of Real Estate, ...	22000
Capital in Trade, ...	13000
He has therefore to *pay interest* on	2000
While H. Boomer *receives interest* on . . .	3000

JOURNAL ENTRIES FOR INTEREST TO PARTNERS.

Ira Mayhew *Dr.*	200	00		
Interest on $2000 @ 10 %				
To Interest			200	00
"				
Interest *Dr.*	300	00		
On $3000 @ 10 %				
To Hiram Boomer			300	00

EXAMPLE IV. CLOSING.

(Page 228.)

After posting the Journal entries for Interest to the partners, we shall be prepared to take the following

Dr. *Trial Balance.* *Cr.*

Dr.			Cr.		
Cash	9875	50	Ira Mayhew	12800	
Bills Receivable	12940		Hiram Boomer	18300	
Expenses	1120		Bills Payable	4600	
Exchange	28	75	Interest	175	80
Merchandise	11911	55			
	35875	80		35875	80

Having entered to the Cr. of Merchandise the value of the amount on hand, per Inventory, we are prepared to make the closing Journal entries required by Art. 305 of Book-keeping, as follows:

Account		Dr.		Cr.	
Sundries Dr.					
Merchandise	Gross Profits	3461	45		
Interest	Gain on	175	80		
To Profit & Loss				3637	25
//					
Profit & Loss Dr.		1148	75		
To Expenses	Amount of			1120	
" Exchange	Loss on			28	75
//					
Profit & Loss Dr.	Net Gain	2488	50		
To Ira Mayhew	His half			1244	25
" Hiram Boomer	His half			1244	25

www.ingramcontent.com/pod-product-compliance
Lightning Source LLC
LaVergne TN
LVHW021421110826
845150LV00007B/2030

* 9 7 8 1 4 2 5 5 0 8 5 4 8 *